New Policy Guidelines for Reading

New Policy Guidelines for Reading

Connecting Research and Practice

Jerome C. Harste
Indiana University

National Council of Teachers of English
1111 Kenyon Road, Urbana, Illinois 61801

ERIC Clearinghouse on Reading and Communication Skills

Staff Editor: Tim Bryant

Book Design: Cover, Michael J. Getz; interior, Tom Kovacs for TGK Design

NCTE Stock Number 33428-3020

Published 1989 by the National Council of Teachers of English and the ERIC Clearinghouse on Reading and Communication Skills. Printed in the United States of America.

This publication was prepared with funding from the Office of Educational Research and Improvement, U.S. Department of Education, under contract no. 400-86-0045. Contractors undertaking such projects under government sponsorship are encouraged to express freely their judgment in professional and technical matters. Prior to publication, the manuscript was submitted to the Editorial Board of the National Council of Teachers of English for critical review and determination of professional competence. This publication has met such standards. Points of view or opinions, however, do not necessarily represent the official view or opinions of either the National Council of Teachers of English or the Office of Educational Research and Improvement.

Library of Congress Cataloging-in-Publication Data

LB
1050.6
.H37
1989

Harste, Jerome C. (Jerome Charles)
    New policy guidelines for reading : connecting research and practice / Jerome C. Harste.
        p.   cm.
    Bibliography: p.
    Includes index.
    ISBN 0-8141-3342-8
    1. Reading—Research—United States.   2. Reading—United States.
I. National Council of Teachers of English.   II. Title.
LB1050.6.H37   1989
428.4'072073—dc19   89-3034
                                                                    CIP

Contents

Foreword

This book was developed during the period when the ERIC Clearinghouse on Reading and Communication Skills (ERIC/RCS) was sponsored by the National Council of Teachers of English. The Educational Resources Information Center (ERIC) is a national information system developed by the U.S. Department of Education and sponsored by the Office of Educational Research and Improvement (OERI). ERIC provides ready access to descriptions of exemplary programs, research and development reports, and related information useful in developing effective educational programs.

Through its network of specialized centers, or clearinghouses, each of which is responsible for a particular educational area, ERIC acquires, evaluates, abstracts, and indexes current significant information and lists this information in its reference publications.

The ERIC system has already made available — through the ERIC Document Reproduction Service — a considerable body of data, including all federally funded research reports since 1956. However, if the findings of educational research are to be used by teachers, much of the data must be translated into an essentially different context. Rather than resting at the point of making research reports readily accessible, OERI has directed the ERIC clearinghouses to commission authorities in various fields to write information analysis papers.

This book, then, is the most recent of dozens of practitioner-oriented texts developed by ERIC/RCS in cooperation with the National Council of Teachers of English. The Clearinghouse and NCTE hope that the materials are helpful in clarifying important educational issues and in improving classroom practice.

Charles Suhor
Deputy Executive Director, NCTE

Introduction

This book is intended to help teachers, researchers, curriculum developers, and administrators develop improved policy in reading instruction and research. The recommendations in this volume evolved from two federally funded studies: a review of trends in instructional research in reading comprehension (Crismore 1985) and a descriptive study of reading comprehension instruction in classrooms (Harste and Stephens 1985).[1]

This document challenges several widespread assumptions about effective reading instruction and concludes with twenty policy guidelines for improving research and instruction in reading. These guidelines evolved from a program of research designed to evaluate current practice in light of, and in contrast to, what researchers think we currently know. In the sense that it attends to practice, this report differs from most previous discussions of public policy on literacy.

Although most issues raised here are ones about which reasonable persons can disagree, this report does take stands based on what appears to be the strongest available evidence. The report and the envisioned policies offer no panaceas, only the promise of progress through collaborative effort and continued willingness to expand our understanding of reading theory and practice.

Reading, Reading Instruction, and Reading Research

It is often implicitly suggested that we could easily solve the problems of teaching reading comprehension if we applied what we know from research. However, before rushing to use research as the sole base for developing instructional policy, it is important to determine the relationship between reading, research on reading, and reading instruction. There are four possible logical relationships which might exist (Beaugrande 1985):

1. The processes are essentially the same.
2. The processes are different from each other.
3. Reading research and reading instruction intensify key elements in real-world reading.
4. The relationship between the three processes is one of reductionism. That is, reading research and reading instruction distort the process of reading.

Same Processes

The first possibility is that reading, research on reading, and reading instruction are one and the same (Figure 1A). This possibility is implausible in light of the fact that reading activities in school often differ from what readers actually do outside of school (Mikulecky 1981, Harste and Mikulecky 1984; see also Dyson 1984, Odell 1980).[2] Because most researchers still use psychology majors to study reading under laboratory conditions — as opposed to studying what readers do under real-world reading conditions — the research community tends to know more about reading under laboratory conditions than under more realistic ones.[3]

It is not surprising that some educators are now calling for more field-based studies rather than traditional laboratory-based research on reading. Others even suggest that one of the fastest ways to set the reading curriculum in order is to throw out all instructional practices not grounded in what real readers or writers do in everyday settings.[4]

3

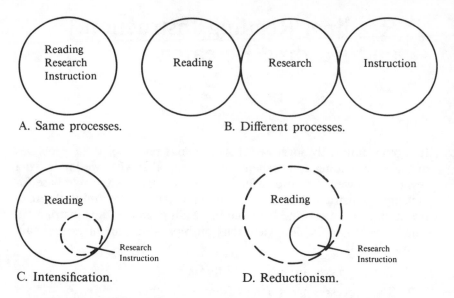

Figure 1. Four possible relationships between reading, reading instruction, and reading research.

Given the gap between laboratory-based reading research and reading in normal social settings, as well as the artificiality of many classroom activities in reading, it seems safe to conclude that whatever the relationship is between reading, reading instruction, and research in reading, the three are not the same.

This conclusion is important. It helps teachers and researchers clarify for themselves and others what they are (or ought to be) about. Many problems arise when we assume that reading instruction is reading, or when we infer that what children do when faced with nonsense words in certain research settings is the same as what they do when faced with print situated in a meaningful context.

Different Processes

A second possibility is that reading instruction, reading, and research on reading are completely different entities (Figure 1B). This possibility suggests that the three processes do not touch, that each constitutes a separate world.

There is some evidence for this possibility, particularly given the aforementioned lack of intersection between reading research and real reading. Yet, in the case of reading and reading instruction, the likelihood of there being no overlap is remote. Despite the ditto sheets and other artifices that dominate reading instruction in many classrooms, to the extent that children are given the opportunity to go to the library to select things they really wish to read or are allowed to write on topics of their own choice in their classrooms, some overlap does exist. Of course, the overlap between reading and reading instruction in some classrooms is greater than in others.

The same can be said about the intersection between research in reading and real-world reading. While readers have rarely been given much choice of reading material under research conditions, for some studies this is not true. In fact, the current trend is toward more ethnographic or field-based studies (Harste 1985b; see also Note 5), and many ethnographic researchers have purposely selected classrooms which simulate natural learning environments. These researchers assume that we might learn more by studying classrooms that are rich reading environments than by studying classrooms in which reading is narrowly defined.

Intensification

The third possibility for the relationship between reading, the study of reading, and reading instruction is that research and instruction intensify certain processes without necessarily distorting them. To envision this possibility, one might conceive of reading as a large circle, with a smaller circle within representing reading instruction or reading research (Figure 1C). This possibility is optimistic. It suggests that the relationship between research, reading, and reading instruction is indeed continuous, differing only in that research and instruction focus on or highlight key processes (but not all processes) within the general area of reading. It also suggests that research and reading instruction differ from real-world reading only in that the first two intensify or focus closely on key cognitive operations in reading.

If the intensification hypothesis is valid, it would mean — given our review of reading comprehension research from the past ten years — that such strategies as inferencing, generalizing, monitoring, and summarizing are key operations in successful reading. Researchers, of course, would love to believe that this is the case. Yet we must be careful. Many key reading strategies — e.g., applying what one knows about letter/sound relationships, about the flow of language, and about how language varies across the circumstances of use — have not been the focus of great numbers of researchers during the past ten years. This is not because these topics are considered unimportant but because their centrality in the reading process has been confirmed and because researchers today think that the potential of these topics for expanding our horizons of knowledge about reading is limited in comparison to the exploration of other aspects of the process.

Having said all this, I still find the intensification perspective useful. Clearly, researchers now know more about the process of reading than ever before. New stances, because they have focused on strategies, process, and comprehension, have advanced our understanding more than past perspectives. There is no doubt in my mind that reading instruction would be greatly improved if we were to apply what researchers have learned about key reading comprehension processes over the past ten years. This does not mean, however, that these processes are all we should teach. Children will still need to go to the library, read widely, and be given daily opportunities to use reading as a tool for exploring and expanding their worlds. And research is continually providing new insights that prompt critical reordering of priorities in instructional practices.

Reductionism

The fourth possibility is that the relationship between reading, reading instruction, and reading research is one of reductionism (Figure 1D). This is much like the intensification possibility, with the noticeable difference that it is less optimistic.

The reductionism possibility posits that rather than intensifying key strategies, reading research and instruction lead to distortions. This is, I believe, a real likelihood. Often our attempts at simplifying reading instruction and shaping researchable hypotheses impose a tidiness that is quite unnatural, given how reading works outside the classroom. Carolyn Burke (1980) reminds us that while we can talk about a complex process simply, doing so does not alter the complexity of the process. Her reminder is useful for both researchers and teachers as they go about translating recent research into practice.

I believe that the reductionism possibility is the most typical relationship between research and practice. There is much evidence for this in recent policy reports on the status of reading. Research topics come and go (as demonstrated by the "hot topics" on annual programs at professional meetings), and a bandwagon effect clearly operates in research as well as in education more generally. Researchers, teachers, and educators would be deluding themselves if they failed to take the reductionism possibility seriously.

The reductionism possibility is also the reason, I think, that the bifurcation between research and practice is neither necessarily healthy nor, over the long run, beneficial to the teaching profession. In this regard, I have called for teachers and researchers to work collaboratively in the development of a practical theory of literacy instruction. Such a theory must be developed in collaboration in classrooms, with teachers and researchers each contributing their expertise. As long as the relationship between research and practice is seen as one-way rather than as dynamic, teachers and researchers both lose. Good teaching is a form of research, and both teaching and research are forms of a continuous learning process. The sooner educators see that they share a common purpose as well as a common goal, the faster revitalization and growth of the teaching profession will occur. Collaborative learning is what both teaching and research are about.

From Theory-to-Practice to Practical Theory

In the realm of policy, this discussion of relationships between reading, reading instruction, and reading research is meant to highlight pitfalls and to caution against simplistic responses to complex issues. Educational policymakers must think in terms of a balanced reading program. A good theory of instruction ought not contradict research findings about the reading process. Yet, because a theory of instruction has to encompass not only reading theory but also writing theory, learning theory, curriculum theory, child growth and development, and more, it necessarily must be broader than research in reading (Goodman 1979).

Many educational researchers do not seem to take this fact into account. My assessment, after reviewing the literature, is that the set of "real" instructional studies — that is, studies that synthesize basic research across a variety of disciplines in an attempt to build and test a theory of instruction in classrooms — is extremely small. Part of the problem is that educational researchers adopt research methodologies from what they see as basic sciences — psychology, sociology, linguistics — rather than attempt to build a methodology of their own which accents synthesis, reflects their goals, and acknowledges the action and charge orientation of their discipline.[5]

The agenda ahead for educators is to develop a research methodology for the discipline of education. They must begin by not being afraid to acknowledge who they are, and by conducting and reporting real educational inquiries in real instructional settings.[6]

In our fieldwork we repeatedly encountered school districts which either had severed relationships with local colleges or universities or had never really developed substantive relationships in the first place. In part, this pattern exists because elementary/secondary school people have bought into the notion that research is something colleges do, while teaching is something schools do. They see college professors of education as being involved in knowledge production, and teachers as being involved in knowledge utilization. The unfortunate effect of such positions is that both groups of educators cut themselves off from ready sources of new knowledge. Instructional theory isn't something one applies to practice; it is the result of an attempt both to explain and to improve practice.

One way to change the currently prevalent pattern would be for each school district in the country to identify a series of demonstration-center classrooms within its borders and to encourage its teachers to align themselves with a reading educator at an institution of higher education who has similar educational interests. The Albuquerque Public School System and the Denver Public School System have already formalized these sorts of arrangements in their area.[7] Other districts have begun to move in this direction, though the university-school relationship is more informal.

Some of the goals public school teachers and college reading experts have begun to explore successfully through these programs are: (1) setting up a theoretically based reading, writing, and thinking curriculum (Harste and Jurewicz 1985, Shanklin and Rhodes 1985, Shanklin and Vacca 1985, Smith et al. 1985),[8] (2) integrating reading and writing in the language arts program of special education students (Stephens 1986), (3) rethinking beginning reading and writing in terms of recent findings about how reading and writing evolve (Pierce 1984, Clyde 1986, Pinnell 1985), (4) developing a literature-based reading and writing program (Short 1986), and (5) exploring how reading lessons might be improved to encourage and support critical thinking (Altwerger and Resta 1985; Au 1980; Au and Mason 1981; Hansen and Graves 1984; Tierney, Pearson, and Tucker 1984; Smith-Burke, personal communication).

Unlike the old model of educational research — in which the researcher gathers a great deal of data but the classroom stays the same — in these projects everyone grows. Often researcher and teacher exchange roles, each contributing what they know. Curriculum is collaboratively constructed by the researcher, teacher, and students involved.

New policy guidelines must actively support the process of educators helping themselves. Policymakers are rightfully interested in the curriculum of the children in the district they serve. They must also become interested in their own curriculum as decision makers, and in that of their teachers as professionals. Educational policies which fail to support learning by everyone — including the student, the teacher, the researcher, the administrator, and the policymaker — are neither educational nor sound. To do otherwise is shortsighted and relegates the teacher to the role of spectator rather than participant in the development of educational research and practice.

Supporting Practical Theory

Districts must begin by supporting teachers and teacher judgment. This call runs counter to the notion that teachers aren't very competent, another assumption underlying many of the recent reports on the status of education in our society.[9] The argument takes many forms: teachers aren't well-prepared; they aren't effective; they don't know how to teach. It is also argued that reading comprehension is rarely taught in schools; mostly, it is tested and corrected (Durkin 1978–79; for other interpretations, see Allington 1984; Gambrell 1984; Neilsen, Rennie, and Connell 1982; Smith and Feathers 1983).

During our field study we were struck by how many administrators, teachers, and school board members have accepted these assumptions and have developed rather restrictive school policies accordingly. Before these assumptions are taken as truth, however, it is important that they be examined carefully.

Trusting Teachers

First, let us examine the notion of whether teachers are effective in their jobs. Probably the most concise and yet most convincing evidence on this point is the body of data about which Diane DeFord reported (DeFord 1981). She asked advocates of three distinct approaches to the teaching of reading to nominate the teacher who they felt most effectively used their preferred approach. She then spent from three to six months in each teacher's classroom collecting reading and writing samples, videotape, audio recordings, and other materials.

Figure 2 shows representative uninterrupted writing excerpts from each classroom. When asked to write, children in the phonics classroom, where phonics was the dominant mode and focus of reading instruction, produced sentences such as "I had a gag," "I had a dad," and "I had a cat."

In the skills classroom, where the focus of beginning reading instruction was on the development of a sight vocabulary through flash cards and simple stories made up of those words, children produced sentences such as "Bill can run," "Jill can run," "Jeff can run," and "I can run."

11

Reed: Phonics Room

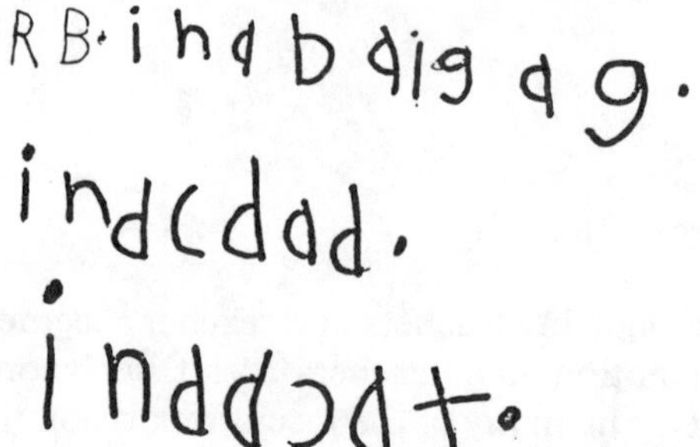

R B · i h ɑ b ɑ i g ɑ g .   (I had a gag.)

i n ɑ c d ɑ d .   (I had a dad.)

i n ɑ d ɔ ɑ t .   (I had a cat.)

Jeffrey and Amy: Skills Room

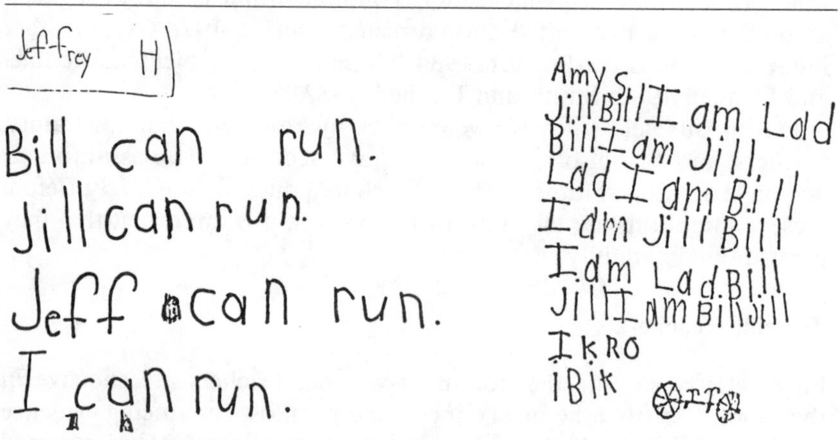

Jeffrey   H)

Bill can run.
Jill can run.
Jeff can run.
I can run.

Amys
Jill Bill I am Lod
Bill I am Jill.
Lod I am Bill
I am Jill Bill
I am Lad Bill
Jill I am Bill Jill
I k RO
IBIK

Jason: Whole Language Room

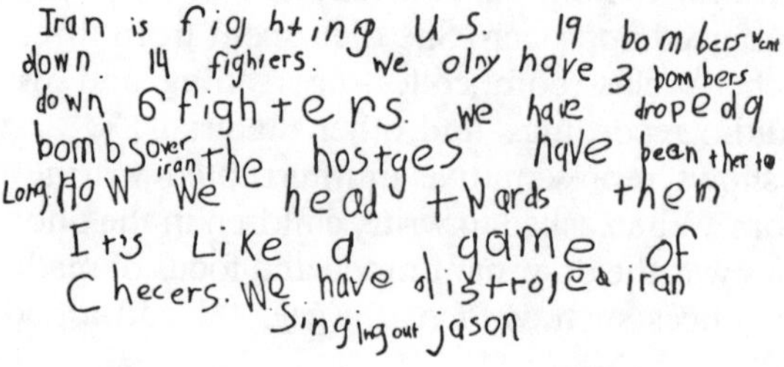

Iran is fighting US. 19 bombers went
down. 14 fighters. We olny have 3 bombers
down 6 fighters. we have droped q
bomb over iran the hostges have bean thr to
Long How We head twards them
Its Like a game of
Checers. We have distrojed iran
Singing out jason

Figure 2. Uninterrupted writing samples from children in classrooms that employ different approaches to reading instruction (DeFord 1981).

In both the phonics classroom and the skills classroom, children limited the content of what they wrote to what they had been taught formally in the classroom. However, the writing looked different in predictable ways. In the phonics classroom, children played with letter/sound patterns. In the skills classroom, on the other hand, children played with words and generated sentences by substituting one known word for another.

This same pattern held for reading. In the phonics classroom, the dominant strategy was sounding out. Children often made multiple attempts at words and produced nonsense words when this strategy failed (e.g., "turntell" for "turtles"). In the skills classroom, children tended to substitute words that had been introduced in instruction for words they perceived to be spelled similarly (e.g., "should" for "sound"; "so" for "she").[10]

Rather than use their own knowledge about language to augment what the teacher was doing, children in both classrooms limited the strategies they used to those the teacher had introduced. Children in both the phonics classroom and the skills classroom assumed, in effect, that what they knew about reading prior to coming to school was no longer useful.

The third classroom that DeFord studied was a whole language classroom. Here children were encouraged to read or pretend to read from the first day of class. Children were taken on an environmental-print walk the first day of school, where they were asked to find something they could read. That evening they were sent home to find packaging they could read in their cupboards and to collect package labels. The teacher then had the children put their labels in a book and write — doing the best they could — anything that they wanted to say about each label. These writings were shared by the authors with their classmates and parents.

In the whole language classroom, instruction in reading began with shared reading. Predictable books, such as *The Three Little Pigs, Little Red Hen, The Great Big Enormous Turnip,* and others, were read orally, first as a group and later individually by the children. Because these stories were familiar, children were invited to chime in whenever they could. They were then encouraged to make books using the patterns of language in the stories that were read.[11]

The third writing sample in Figure 2 is typical of the children in this first-grade classroom. In this instance, Jason was playing the role of reporter. His newspaper article gives a status report on United States–Iran relations. In contrast to the other samples, Jason's story is striking. Unlike the children in the phonics and skills classrooms, Jason uses a wide range of vocabulary, varied sentence structure, and prior knowledge about reporting to get his article to sound like an actual newspaper article.

DeFord could find no evidence at the start of the year that the groups of children in the three classrooms differed fundamentally from one another in background.[12] Given the pervasive influence of mode of instruction on student output, however, direct comparisons are difficult. The strategies used by each group of children directly reflected the strategies taught in their instructional settings. In the classroom where children were invited to test a wide set of hypotheses, they essentially did so; in the classrooms where the strategies of instruction were limited, the children's strategies reflected those restrictions.

One general point which these data suggest is that instruction is effective. While we may prefer what children do in some classrooms over and above what they do in others, the overall trend is important: children learn what their teachers teach.[13] A second implication of these data is more subtle, but equally important: children tend to use instructional strategies in the way they are taught.

Our extended observations in a wide variety of classrooms and our reading of hundreds of research reports led us to concur with these findings. In classroom after classroom, children confirmed the patterns. In one instructional study after another, the patterns continued. Findings confirmed that any instructional treatment is effective. If phonics is stressed, children do well on phonics tests. If vocabulary development is stressed, children do well on vocabulary tests. If inferencing is studied, children do well on measures of inference. If children are asked to apply their knowledge in ways different from the way in which it was originally taught, they do less well than children taught and tested on parallel forms (King 1985).

The issue, then, is not whether instruction is effective, but — if anything — whether or not it is *too* effective. This evidence suggests that teachers take teaching seriously, and that children take their teachers seriously. The real issue is not teacher competency but whether we are teaching children what we ought to be teaching in the name of literacy. This is a quite different, but more pertinent, issue.

Supporting Inquiry

If children do indeed learn what we teach, setting up the most effective classroom environment becomes important. Anthropologist Shirley Brice Heath (in press) argues that the following behaviors are deemed by our society as characterizing a critical thinker:

1. A critical thinker acts out of a disposition to think and speak as an individual pitting his or her judgments against those of another individual or individuals.

2. A critical thinker may counter, complement, compare, or supplement information given by others as well as appraise the manner of construction of facts others use to present the information.

3. A critical thinker lays claim to a specific knowledge base out of which assertions and counter-assertions to the knowledge presented by others are made. Thus, one who acts as a critical thinker takes on a social role that calls for frequent verbal displays of knowledge.

4. A critical thinker both assesses an ongoing exchange and projects a mental image of a sequenced future situation, moving back and forth between the current scene and the mentally constructed future outcome of the ongoing process.

5. A critical thinker focuses on the actual process of reflective thinking about a subject, action, or problem. Critical thinking is thinking about thinking while in the very process of expressing one's thoughts.

Sociolinguists and psycholinguists suggest that we participate our way into literacy. To be successful, language learners assess the context of the situation in which they find themselves and produce a text that they see as reasonable or appropriate. Researchers have found that poor readers are often in trouble because they take the teacher too seriously. These readers suffer from an "instructionally dependent attitude" — trying only those strategies and techniques that were explicitly taught and nothing more (Board 1981).

While the readers in DeFord's study were not in trouble, a game-like process was quite evident. That is, they played the phonics game, the skills game, and so on. If the children in the phonics classroom were suddenly placed in the whole language classroom, we can safely assume that they not only would need, but indeed would learn how, to play the new game.

Children as language learners are survivors. When constraints change, so do the learners' language and performance. Understanding this basic process in literacy learning makes the reading programs we design all the more important. In light of current knowledge, such programs ought to focus on comprehension. Linguists, for example, tell us that meaning is what language is all about. Without meaning, language is nonsense. No one reads to sound out words; no one writes to see how many words they can spell correctly. Reading and writing are social events which have as their purposes communication and learning (Beaugrande 1980, 1981; Beaugrande and Dressler 1981; Bruce 1979;

Dillon 1978; van Dijk 1976; Gollasch 1982a, 1982b; Halliday 1973a, 1973b, 1974, 1978; Holdaway 1979; Mischler 1979; Shuy 1979; Smith 1978).

Reading research reveals that competent readers (1) read for meaning; (2) monitor their reading even as they read; (3) are critical rather than accepting of what they read; and (4) summarize, generalize, and try to make sense of what they are reading in light of their prior knowledge (Anderson, Spiro, and Montague 1977; Bussie 1982; Brown 1977, 1981, 1982; Brown and Smiley 1977; van Dijk 1977, 1979; Gollasch 1982a, 1982b; Pearson 1984; Sherman 1979; Spiro, Bruce, and Brewer 1980; Winograd 1983; Winograd et al. 1984; Winograd and Johnston 1982). It is clear that while these processes vary in specific detail among individuals, they are universals in reading (see above; see also Smith 1978; Gollasch 1982a, 1982b). It is also clear that reading is driven by a search for a unified meaning or text (see above; see also Goodman 1984, Iser 1978).

Reading researchers define reading as the process of constructing meaning through a dynamic interaction between the reader's existing knowledge, the information suggested by the written language, and the context of the reading situation (Seminoff, Wixson, and Peters 1984).[14] This definition emphasizes the interactive, constructive, and dynamic nature of the reading process. The term *interactive* indicates that reading is an act of communication dependent not only on the knowledge and skill of the author but on the knowledge and skill of the reader as well. The term *constructive* signifies that meaning is something that cannot simply be extracted from a text but rather must be actively created in the mind of the reader from the integration of prior knowledge with the information suggested by the text. The term *dynamic* emphasizes that the reading process is variable, not static, and adapts to the specific demands of each particular reading experience. This definition thus recognizes that reading will vary from situation to situation, and that skilled reading is strategic — involving the ability to tailor one's activities to the demands of each reading situation (Kirsch and Guthrie 1985, Smith 1978).

The above definition contrasts quite drastically with a definition of reading one might infer from observing classroom instruction. While there are some classrooms that focus children's attention on comprehension and meaning, and no classrooms which totally ignore comprehension, more could and should be done to stress comprehension in most classrooms.

Effective Reading Comprehension Instruction

In the classrooms we observed (Harste and Stephens 1985) that emphasized comprehension, trade books were readily available and uninterrupted time was scheduled for students to read and discuss critically the relationship of their selections to a topic of interest they were studying. Good comprehension instruction seemed to be planned to permit activity (time to read, time to engage) as well as reflexivity (time to discuss what was learned, time to discuss which reading strategies were or were not useful).

In the settings that did not center on comprehension, vocabulary study replaced real reading and discussions were kept to a minimum and at a literal level. In many of these classrooms children encountered more words on worksheets than they did in books. In all too many low-reading groups, children were not encouraged to think critically, nor was critical thinking demonstrated to the children by the teacher. This omission was particularly serious since these children were ability-grouped and hence had no opportunity to benefit from learning from more successful readers. In some instances the assumption that children could not read led teachers to design lessons which permitted children to circumvent reading as a tool for learning. (In contrast, Figure 3 shows a sampling of reading materials that a group of seventh graders labeled learning disabled read on their own.[15]) In too many classrooms reading was treated as a silent, private act which one must master on one's own. When the program was "individualized," no discussion was possible because everyone was working on separate reading assignments. Discussion and collaboration were seen as forms of "cheating," as opposed to forms of support.

In supportive classrooms, the more successful readers were paired with less successful readers and children were encouraged to talk their way through the reading with a partner. The focus was on making meaning and on sharing understandings with peers during and after reading. Class discussions synthesized insights and helped students search for and construct a unified meaning. Children were asked to reflect on what they had learned as well as to identify what they still had to find out. Reading comprehension instruction in these classrooms reflected recent insights into comprehension and learning. There is no doubt that reading instruction would be greatly improved in most classrooms if we would only apply current findings about reading comprehension in the design of instructional activities.

BILLIE JEAN KING

"Women should not play tennis," said Bobby Riggs. "Women should stay at home. Tennis is a man's game." That is what many people thought, years ago. They did not want to watch women play. Men were the exciting players. But that was before Billie Jean King. Billie Jean proved that women could be as exciting to watch as men. When she played everyone was amazed at how good she was. She won the big matches at Wimbledon and Forest Hills many times.

Olivia Newton-John

Olivia Newton-John, who grew up in Australia, loved two things as a child—animals and music. She was always bringing home stray or injured dogs and cats. Her mother, however, was afraid of dogs, and since her family lived where no pets were allowed, Olivia could not have pets of her own.

When Olivia was fourteen, music became her major interest. She formed a singing trio with two other girls. The very next year she won a talent contest. First prize was a trip to London. Without a second thought, Olivia quit school and flew to England to begin a serious career in music.

Now one of the best-liked pop-country singers in the world, Olivia has recorded many albums. She has received four Grammy awards. After making her first movie, *Grease*, with John Travolta, Olivia became a movie star as well as a recording artist. Since then, she has also made videos and television specials. Her career as an entertainer is very different from being either a mounted police officer or a veterinarian, the two careers she chose as a child.

© 1987. Educational Insights, Inc., Dominguez Hills, CA.

FRANKENSTEIN

Mary Shelley

Victor Frankenstein was born in Geneva, Switzerland. He was the oldest son of a wealthy Swiss family. Victor's childhood was happy. His parents were loving and kind to him and his two younger brothers, Ernest and William. Victor's classmate, Henry Clerval, was a loyal friend. Victor had a sweetheart, Elizabeth Lavenza. They looked forward to the day when they would marry.

When Victor was seventeen, he went to a German school to study science. He liked the subject. Soon he knew as much as his teachers. Victor began to study on his own. He wanted to discover the secret of life. When that goal was reached, he would create life itself!

After much study, Victor learned the secret of life. "Now that I know this secret," he thought, "I will use it to give life to the lifeless!" Victor began to collect materials for his work. At night he went to medical laboratories. He went to alleys behind butcher shops. He took bodies from grave-yards. All that he found was brought back to his own laboratory. There, he set to work creating a man.

Frankenstein worked hard for many months. Finally his creature was ready. But it was not yet alive. Using electricity, Frankenstein brought his creation to life.

The creature's eyes opened and his arms and legs moved. Frankenstein was suddenly filled with horror. He had meant for his creature to be beautiful. But once it was alive, the scientist saw that it was ugly and horrible. The creature's eyes were pale, his skin was shriveled, and his lips were black.

Frankenstein fled the room in terror and disgust. He did not realize that the creature was really kind and gentle.

Saddened by the horror he had caused, the creature left the laboratory. He hid in the woods. He warmed himself at deserted fires. Berries and nuts were his food. But the creature wished to learn about humans, and to live among them.

Figure 3. Children in a junior high special education classroom worked collaboratively to read these passages.

Curricular Guidelines from Research

There are three important curricular guidelines which emanate from research in linguistics and reading comprehension. The first is that there is no way to learn a process other than through engaging in that process. Over and over again research shows that providing time and a supportive environment for critical reading leads to children reading critically, that encouraging inferencing leads to better inferencing, that opportunities to summarize lead to growth in summarizing, and so on (see Rowe 1985a, 1985b).[16] This means that our curriculum must include time to work on comprehension because children must have ongoing opportunities to use the strategies we associate with successful readers and writers. These opportunities can come in the form of daily incentives to do real reading and writing for real purposes. Even in more restrictive environments, however, an expanded list of comprehension skills could easily be generated and lists of skills inverted so that reading for meaning precedes such skills work as phonics, word meaning, and the recall of detail — activities which now consume so much time that teachers and children seldom deal with the strategies involved in making sense of reading, or comprehension. One first-grade teacher told us, "Meaning? We don't get to that until the end of the year and sometimes not even then!"

The second curricular insight is that much of what anyone knows about such activities as reading, writing, and critical thinking is learned from being in the presence of others engaged in these processes rather than from direct instruction (Smith 1978, 1982, 1984).[17] With respect to curriculum, this observation implies that it is important for children not only to engage in reading, writing, and thinking but to have opportunities to share, discuss with, and be around more proficient readers and writers.

Under ideal conditions, reading and writing are presented as functional, collaborative events enhanced through active participation and partnership. Thus, in the most dynamic classrooms we observed, school administrators came in and read with children, teachers read and wrote in front of and with children, and sharing times and young author conferences were an integral part of curriculum.

The third guideline is that a good curriculum not only provides opportunities to engage in and see demonstrated the strategies of successful written language use and learning, but also provides opportunities to come to value these strategies. Part of this valuing comes as a function of engagement. Another part comes from being immersed in a community of readers and writers. A third part is more deliberate —

it is an attempt to bring aspects of the engagement process to a level of conscious awareness.[18] Researchers are uncertain about the extent to which readers and writers are aware of the strategies they use, so for instructional purposes it is probably enough that children be invited to talk about what tactics work and don't work when they are reading a book, interpreting a poem, or working on a research report. In sharing, children get confirmation, find out what options are available, and discover what new strategies might be tried. Constructive teachers use the anomalous response as an invitation for the group to grow ("Tommy said that he 'argued with the author' as he read. . . . Why don't we all try to do that when we read the next section?").

If what learners value is not confirmed by others, then knowledge atrophies. For example, after only twenty days of phonics instruction, children we studied (Harste, Woodward, and Burke 1984) had abandoned every other reading strategy except sounding out words — even though at ages three, four, and five they had used a much wider and more powerful set of strategies. Teachers in our classroom practice study (Harste and Stephens 1985) often talked about good instructional practices which they had once used but which they'd since abandoned.

Taking Risks

The average reading proficiency levels of nine-, thirteen-, and seventeen-year-olds in each of four national assessments provide an accurate index of national trends in reading achievement (NAEP 1985):

> During the past 13 years, the reading proficiency of 9-year-old students has improved significantly. . . .
>
> Thirteen-year-olds too are reading significantly better than they were in 1971, but this improvement has not been as dramatic across assessments. . . .
>
> Trends in achievement for 17-year-olds differ markedly from those for the other two age groups. Throughout the 1970s, the reading proficiency level of the 17-year-olds was remarkably constant, but this was followed by a significant improvement between 1980 and 1984. (pp. 9–10)

Despite these accomplishments, the authors of this report and others (Farr and Fay 1982; Farr, Fay, and Negley 1978; Goodman 1983; Stitch 1983, 1985) have concluded that while we have made improvements in teaching "basic skills," we have not been successful in teaching "higher-level comprehension skills" and critical thinking. The authors of *The Reading Report Card* summarize current thinking as well as provide guidance to teachers and researchers:

There has been a conceptual shift in the way many researchers and teachers think about reading, which gives students a much more active role in the learning and reading comprehension process. This shift is reflected in changes from packaged reading programs to experiences with books and from concentration on isolated skills to practical reading and writing activities.

Yet, improvements in higher-level reading skills cannot come about simply by an emphasis on reading instruction in isolation from the other work students do in school. To foster higher-level literacy skills is to place a new and special emphasis on thoughtful, critical elaboration of ideas and understandings drawn from the material students read and from what they already know. They must learn to value their own ideas and to defend as well as question their interpretations in the face of alternative or opposing points of view.

The development of such thoughtful, creative approaches to learning runs counter to much of what students are asked to do in school. Reading in schools is sometimes a relatively superficial activity, a prelude to a recitation of what others have said. Though not optimal, such approaches may be sufficient when teachers are most concerned with the "right" answer and lower-level skills. At other times, reading can be a thoughtful, creative activity, one that challenges students to extend and elaborate upon what others have said or written. In developing higher-level reading skills and strategies, students will benefit from experience with a wide range of challenging materials. Though there has been considerable concern with providing students with "readable" texts — and a concomitant simplification of instructional materials — this may have inadvertently reduced students' opportunities to develop comprehension strategies for dealing with more complicated material that presents new ideas.

There are opportunities for such experiences in all of the subjects students study in school, as well as in what they read at home. They can learn to develop their own interpretations of what they read, to question, rethink, and elaborate upon the ideas and information drawn from their reading experiences — in conversations with their friends, in discussions with their teachers, and in the writing they do for themselves and others. And in that process, students will also be acquiring the higher-level reading comprehension skills that so many are presently lacking. (pp. 8–9)

Universal public education never will be easy, nor will it be cheap. This does not mean that we must condone the current state of education or the state of literacy in the United States.[19] We have not done badly; we simply could do a whole lot better by applying what we currently know and by using this as a base upon which to grow.

Because of the tenor of our times — times that feed the assumptions implicit in the belief that teachers of reading are not very effective — the demands of comprehension and critical thinking are on us all. This includes students, to be sure, but also teachers, researchers, curriculum developers, administrators, and school board members. Rather than react from a position of defense, we need to respond from a position of strength. Educational policy should be designed using progress as its metaphor and should be a supportive attempt to marshal and use teachers as a resource in the revitalization of education. This is best done by seeing opportunity rather than fault and by thinking collaboration.

For teachers, researchers, curriculum developers, school board members, and administrators, this is no time for conservatism. Teachers and researchers should be supported in their efforts to keep informed and should be encouraged to test their best hypotheses as to how to create a conducive environment for classroom reading instruction.

The effort might begin by legitimizing teacher insight (Snyder 1985). During our observations of classroom reading instruction, we found that whenever the teacher "stepped out" (that is, included things in the program beyond those recommended in the available commercial program) these innovations were better, from a theoretical perspective, than were those advocated by the published program. For example, Mrs. B used a highly structured reading program (Chicago Mastery Learning 1980) throughout the morning. In an interview she complained that the program was too structured, and that it required some modifications in order to work in her classroom. Because the program called for a great deal of one-on-one teaching, Mrs. B began the day by telling the children about the seatwork they were to complete before joining the reading group. While most of this work had to do with the commercial program the district had adopted (worksheets of one sort or another), Mrs. B always invited the children to write their own stories as an additional seatwork assignment. She would typically use a story starter such as "If I had a million dollars I would . . .," which the children were to complete. Since this activity was unlike any other activity in the name of reading instruction I saw in her classroom, I asked why she included it. She responded,

> Well, I just think it is important that children learn to express their own ideas and have fun in the process. . . . At the end of the morning, we share what we have written. . . . I don't correct the spelling on these papers. . . . We work on spelling at other times. . . . I know a lot of people think these kids can't write. . . . But I tell them to do the best they can . . . and all that is important is that they can read it to be able to share it with the group. . . . I don't know if I am right, but the kids do love it.

In light of current research knowledge, there is much that is right with Mrs. B's activity. Children are asked to use reading and writing functionally. The activity is open-ended, unlike the worksheets. This aspect allows children to enter and exit at different levels — children who are capable of producing only one sentence can do so, while others who are capable of doing more are free to test their skills. Further, the children are cognitively active. They must think critically. They have to use what they know about language to complete the task and, in the process, to orchestrate their knowledge of letter/sound relationships, spelling, the flow of language, and meaning. Recent research in reading, then, would clearly support this activity, whereas it would lend little support to the fragmentation of the process that was taking place in the name of reading instruction as packaged in the commercially available materials adopted by the district.

It is clear that Mrs. B feels vulnerable by including the innovative activity in her program. Because she is not aware of the research base, the writing activity which I believe to be the best part of her program is unfortunately likely to be eliminated with the next classroom demand. Intuitively she did not like the Mastery Learning materials and approach, but because it was the district's adopted program she was more confident in her decision to follow this program in her classroom.

Over and over again the same pattern emerged in our field study of classroom reading instruction. Over and over again teacher intuition was on the right track. But because of recent attacks by the public, teachers felt vulnerable and under these conditions were less likely to follow their intuitions. This is unfortunate. Administrators, school board members, curriculum supervisors, and researchers would do well to help teachers regain their professional confidence. Clearly, without the active participation and intuitions of our most innovative reading educators, reading instruction will not improve as rapidly as it might or should. Teachers and researchers often have quite different concerns. However, to make the progress that we must to develop a theory of reading instruction, teacher involvement, insight, and intuitions are crucial. Our classroom observations suggest that unless our knowledge is turned into creative classroom practice, little real progress is made. Just as what a new definition of reading changes in classrooms is not a bad criterion for judging what difference the new theory makes, so too the criterion for judging new policy guidelines must rest with what real changes they result in.

Experimental Studies in Reading Comprehension

Almost anything teachers do beyond a basal reading program significantly improves reading comprehension. We were charged, for purposes

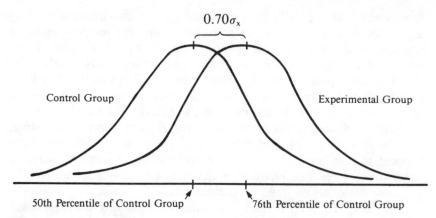

Figure 4. Children receiving an experimental treatment in reading instruction experienced an average gain effect of 0.70 over groups using a basal reading program.

of improving practice, to study what the teaching profession knows about reading comprehension instruction (Crismore 1985). To this end we located and read 525 studies. Many of these studies compared the progress of groups of children receiving an experimental treatment to the progress of other children using the basal reader as their instructional program (see Rowe 1985a).

Figure 4 compares the average score of the experimental treatment group and contrasts it with the average score of the regular basal reading group across a variety of studies and assessment instruments. Students in experimental programs scored more than two-thirds of a standard deviation higher than the control or basal reading groups to which they were compared. This difference is significant. Considering the kind of educational gains we have come to expect in our students, the experimental group's scores represent almost a full year's growth over and above children who participated in only the regular reading program.

One interpretation of these data is the message to teachers and researchers that they should do something new. We coded each of the 525 studies in terms of what aspects of the reading process were being studied. These included text factors, reader factors, task or instructional factors, and processing factors. To understand the full significance of this message, it is important to have some understanding of the range of studies subsumed in this finding:

Text studies included those that attempted in one way or another to make the material used in reading instruction more comprehensible. Research studies that we coded as highlighting text factors looked at the effects of the following: adding subheadings to content-area materials, getting children to create their own subheadings in texts, using predictable reading materials in beginning reading instruction, providing illustrations to aid readability, and helping children develop a conceptual map of the materials they read as an aid to comprehension. Despite the variety, these various practices averaged a .77 gain effect over and above regular reading instruction.[20]

Reader studies highlighted reader factors rather than text factors. Research coded as highlighting the reader included studies that attempted to get readers to bring background information to the reading process, studies which used culturally relevant materials as the basis of reading instruction, and studies which allowed children to choose their own reading materials based on personal interest. Again, despite the variety of ways in which the reader was highlighted and focused upon, the average gain effect for experimental treatments over and above control groups was .60 of one standard deviation.[21]

Task studies included those that attempted to alter the instructional environment or the typical instructional procedures used in basals. These studies involved the use of groups and group discussion as an aid to comprehension, lesson frameworks which attempted to get teachers systematically to activate student background knowledge prior to reading, and various means of enriching the literacy environment of the classroom. Included in the last category were studies in which the functional nature of reading and writing activities was addressed. Researchers in these studies attempted to make the reading and writing tasks in classrooms more functional or more immediately practical for children. Children read and did research on topics of interest to them, and reading and writing were often integrated. Students kept journals, wrote letters, sent notes, and engaged in other natural uses of reading and writing. Other studies purposely expanded the print environments beyond those normally introduced to children in the name of reading and writing instruction. In these studies children were introduced to content-area materials earlier, wrote their own reading materials, or shared literature they had chosen to read. For studies exploring aspects of the instructional task environment, the overall gain effect was .69.[22]

Processing studies attempted to get readers to engage in higher-level cognitive processing. In some studies children were encouraged to monitor meaning as they read, draw inferences, make analogies between the content of their reading and some other familiar experience, create metaphors as an aid to comprehension, engage in mental imagery, and in some cases even recast their understanding of a text in terms of other modes of expression such as drama or art. Instructional studies which focused on higher levels of processing showed, on the average, a large gain effect of 1.04.[23]

In interpreting the above data it is important to remember that for the most part the instructional procedures we studied were theoretically based — that is, grounded in terms of newly perceived insights into the reading process. While it appears that anything new in the classroom results in a gain effect over and above business as usual, it is important to remember that the "anythings" we studied are not mere novelties; they are firmly rooted in our knowledge base.

Most of the studies mentioned above, however, were experimental studies: the researcher manipulated only one variable in each study. We found it surprising that under such conditions so much gain effect occurred.

Collaborative Research Studies

Collaborative studies involve even greater changes than experimental studies (Erickson 1985; Guba and Lincoln 1985a, 1985b). In a collaborative research study, the researcher spends much time in classrooms (typically a semester or more), works with the classroom teacher, and collaborates with the teacher systematically to alter the learning environment. While there are often differences between experimental and ethnographic/collaborative studies in the criterion measures used, there is nonetheless some evidence that under collaborative research conditions the gain effect is larger — often twice as much as that reported in experimental studies. To some extent this follows logically, because collaborative studies involve significantly altering the learning environment as well as the levels of expectation of both teachers and pupils. In one Texas study in which the researcher worked with two first-grade teachers for over a year, children in the experimental classrooms achieved almost two years' gain effect over children at the same grade level in the same school following a more traditional program (Pierce 1984). A Michigan study reported that first-grade children who were asked to write as part of their reading program outscored children in a phonics-only program on the phonics subsection of a standardized reading achievement test (Milz 1984).

Because the amount of directly comparable data is limited, conclusions are difficult to reach. It is worth noting that these gain effects are, however, conservative measures. They fail to capture reported changes in children's attitudes toward reading and writing, as well as the enthusiasm and excitement found in these classrooms by teachers and children alike.

The encouraging trend in instructional research these days is that new researchers entering the field are moving increasingly toward collaboration. Often the classrooms that have been used as research sites are becoming demonstration centers, which other teachers can visit to get ideas and see new programs in operation. While the inservice benefits of these programs have not been measured, the benefits are clearly worth the study and consideration of school districts. As more and more of this research is completed, a clearer picture of the overall instructional and professional effects will become evident.

Building upon What We Know

More innovative thinking about reading has taken place within the last ten to fifteen years than in the previous fifty (see Crismore 1985, Harste 1985b, NAEP 1985). During this period several powerful theoretical models of reading have been developed. Because of the interdisciplinary nature of reading, more scientists are studying the reading process today than ever before. No wonder there has been an explosion of knowledge.

One key factor leading many researchers to question a skills approach to reading instruction was the observation of real readers, outside of academic settings, reading passages and stories. Words understood in one context because they were predictable were not understood in other contexts in which the reader did not expect to find them (Goodman 1965). Rather than reading word-by-word, the most skillful readers made predictions and used a variety of strategies such as skipping words, asking themselves "Did this make sense?" and reading ahead (Goodman 1969, Smith 1971).

Subskills models of reading are based on adult views of skilled reading. There are no ethnographic studies of reading that verify a subskills model of reading instruction.

Researchers also found that what readers brought to the reading situation strongly affected what they got out of the reading selection.[24] Unlike the worksheets developed under skills approaches, in which it was assumed that every adept reader would get the same understanding from a reading experience, variability in reading came to be the expected. Readers, it was discovered, come to the text with a wide variety of different experiences and interests which affect what they get out of the reading experience (Anderson et al. 1977; Carey, Harste, and Smith 1981). Reading is not so much a process of extracting meaning from text as it is making meaning from text.

Reading came to be viewed as a socio-psycholinguistic process rather than as a prescribed set of skills or a product (Bruce 1979, Harste 1980, Tierney and LaZansky 1981). Researchers became interested in the mental activities involved in reading comprehension and interpretation. The criterion for being a successful reader of a narrative was not what was recalled but rather the mental trip or lived-through experience that the reader had while reading the text (Harste and Carey 1979; Rosenblatt 1969, 1978; Shanklin 1981).

These insights led researchers to propose that the outcome of reading is critical thinking — not just a new set of facts (see Short 1985; see also Kintsch and van Dijk 1978, Kintsch 1977). In this framework, good readers were cognitively active, not passive. Reading, like writing, was a tool for thinking — not just for perceiving but for re-perceiving, for thinking, rethinking, and growing (Kucer 1983, Jensen 1984, Pearson and Tierney 1984, Shanklin 1981).

The position that seems to be currently evolving in the field of reading research is that in the final analysis our interest in reading and writing is an interest in learning (see Smith 1980). This position has many practical implications, the majority of which still must be explored and operationalized in classrooms.

Debbie was one student we observed in our field studies (Harste and Stephens 1985). Her reading and retelling of a science article is a good instance of the practical difference between a skills model and a tool-for-learning model of reading. Debbie had read a selection on atoms, which she pronounced /ā-tŏms/ throughout her reading. She was asked to retell what she had read. While her retelling is not very good in terms of her recall of facts, it is an illuminating example of how Debbie is using reading to rethink, to grow, and to expand:

> It was about atoms. . . . I don't know. . . . They're power-ful. . . . Energy, sort of battery-like things. . . . 'Cause it can. . . . No, a battery couldn't take a boat back and forth across the ocean lots of times. . . . There's a big boat, I forgot to mention that. . . . Atoms can sail a big boat with only a little bit of fuel back and forth lots of times. . . . I doubt it!

Debbie is a very active and critical reader. While she didn't get a lot of facts out of the piece, her retelling shows that she tried to integrate what she read with what she knew (see Pearson 1984). Debbie makes the association between atoms and batteries, the closest thing in her experience that seems to make sense. We see her applying background knowledge, testing hypotheses, and reflexively rethinking what she read against what she knows. The mental trip in which she is engaged shows that we need not worry about Debbie as a reader. She employs powerful strategies, and while they don't guarantee a particular product, the process in which she is engaged will ensure growth and learning in the future.

The reader behaviors we value are a function of the model of reading we hold as well as the instructional materials we use and the experiences we plan. To this end, new instructional materials and procedures in reading often reflect new insights into the reading process (see Busch 1985; Dahl and Roberts 1985; Heine 1985; Rowe 1985a; Short 1985, 1986; Stephens 1985). In instructional programs designed to reflect our current knowledge base, high-quality children's literature replaces basal reading stories. Content-area books are introduced to children at an earlier age, newspapers become part of classroom life, and poetry is shared. Cooking centers introduce children to environmental print and the special forms of literacy involved in reading recipes and being a successful cook.

In many current reading programs, writing is no longer seen as a separate subject. Writing, like reading, is viewed as a tool for thinking.[25] In such classrooms, children not only read fairy tales but write their own. Throughout the day children are given opportunities to use writing as a vehicle for sorting out and clarifying their thinking. Reading and writing are used functionally. Rather than play the teacher's game, children actively use reading and writing to explore and expand their growing understanding of topics of interest to them. Even kindergarten children do surveys, compile books of their favorite songs, read predictable books, and explore reading, writing, art, music, and dance as forms of expression.

Today the trend in some classrooms, as well as in the research community more generally, is to see reading and writing as tools for learning. One does not learn to read and then later read to learn; rather, every instance of reading affords the opportunity to learn reading (that is, experience its social and personal usefulness and power), to learn about reading (that is, learn how to do it — what strategies to employ in each particular setting), and to learn through reading (to grow, change, and learn).[26] Authoring is being used as a metaphor for understanding both reading and writing (see Rowe and Harste 1985, Harste and Jurewicz 1985, Short 1986, Stephens 1985, Scibior 1987).

Textbooks

In upper elementary school, middle school, and senior high school, multiple textbooks in a single class are encouraged. In responding to the National Commission on Excellence in Education report *A Nation at Risk* (1983), the International Reading Association published the following policy guideline:

> No single textbook can be geared to the needs of all students. This circumstance does not imply the need for writing new textbooks for poor readers. The existing market contains a plethora of texts which vary in their content, complexity, and cognitive expectations. New uses of available texts are needed. If teachers are expert enough to present model lessons which include phrases such as prior knowledge activation, concept vocabulary development, purpose settings, development of conceptual interrelationships, and reinforcement of learning, students will have the foundation for learning from different texts in the same course. Developing the capability for using multiple texts in one class and sustaining students' strategies for learning from these texts is a challenge to the professionalism of teachers and the ingenuity of teacher educators. (Research Department, IRA, p. 16)

Evaluations of textbooks are frequently based on readability formulas. Although these formulas, which contain variables of sentence length and word difficulty, manifest a gross correlation with the ease with which students learn from texts, they are insufficient.[27] Important factors that are neglected in the use of these formulas include student interest, the number and suitability of concrete examples, clearly stated ideas in a predictable organizational pattern, and a conceptual compatibility with the prior knowledge and experience of students. One aid to textbook evaluation is a readability checklist formulated by Irwin and Davis and published in the *Journal of Reading* (Irwin and Davis 1980). The questions it suggests teachers ask themselves, taking into account the student's familiarity with particular topics and in light of the student's background of experience, include the following:

> Are assumptions about students' vocabulary knowledge appropriate?
> Are assumptions about students' prior knowledge of this content area appropriate?
> Are concepts explicitly linked to students' prior knowledge or to their experiential backgrounds?
> Does the text or teacher's manual provide lists of accessible resources containing alternative readings for the very poor or very advanced readers?
> Is the writing style of the text appealing to the students?
> Are there discussion questions which encourage critical and creative thinking?
> Is there something to learn from reading this text? Does the text contain enough new information so that the student will find it worth reading? (pp. 129–30)

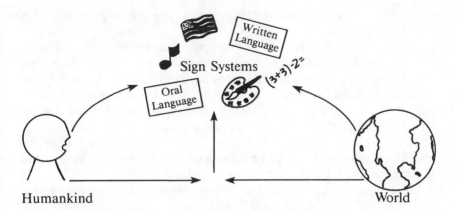

Figure 5. Our perceptions of the world are mediated through sign systems such as music, mathematics, and the language arts.

Questions such as these are important because, given the predominance of poorly conceived textbooks, many children might never understand what it means to be literate or take ownership of the literacy process. Researchers and teachers are concerned that children will fail to experience what reading is all about. They are concerned that children will fail to understand that reading is not just a skill but a way of outgrowing one's current self, a tool for lifelong learning.

Education as the Study of Sign Systems

It is also common today to find reading researchers exploring writing, and writing researchers exploring reading.[28] From the perspective of learning, reading and writing have much in common. In fact, this discovery has led researchers to step further and further back. Some have even felt it necessary to rethink the role reading plays in a system of knowledge (see Harste and Mikulecky 1985, Rowe and Harste 1985, Suhor 1984, Siegel 1983). This has caused some educators to rethink what we mean by "education." Such work has powerful implications for how we think about and teach reading.

One way in which education is currently being redefined is as the study of the process by which we mediate our world for purposes of exploration and expansion (Figure 5).[29] Since we do not have direct access to our world (all that hits our eyes are impulses of light), we create sign systems such as written language, oral language, art, music, mathematics, dance, and the like. These systems are fictions, constructs of our imagination, but they allow us to explore our world. It is through them that we mediate our world and in so doing fundamentally alter it as we explore it.

We now know that atoms, for example, do not really exist. They are a figment of some scientist's imagination. Yet as a construct, the notion that the world is composed of atoms has been helpful. It has allowed us to understand our world, to grow, to develop an atomic bomb, to win a war, to expand our notion of energy. Today, physicists tell us that quarks, not atoms, are the smallest things on earth. To change our knowledge base, old signs — in this case, atoms — had to be abandoned and a new construct had to be developed. We have yet to know what this new construct will allow us to understand.

Education, by this view, is the study of the process of sign production and use. To be really educated is to have an understanding not only of what signs have been produced by past generations and where these constructs have gotten us, but also to have an understanding of the role of sign production in learning (see Suhor 1984, Siegel 1983). Children must not only experience this process but also learn to be reflexive, so that they can outgrow past generations as well as their current selves.[30] To have access to education is to have access to the processes of learning, signification, and reflexivity.

Figure 6 is an example of mediation through sign systems. It is the writing of Megan, age four, whom we asked to write her name and anything else that she could write (Harste, Burke, and Woodward 1981). She drew a picture of herself, wrote her name, wrote the number 4 (her age), and drew four flowers. By so doing Megan demonstrated that she has access to the process of literacy. Megan used a variety of symbols to signify and explore who she is. It is upon this base that effective school programs can be built. As this example illustrates, such programs support children in using and exploring processes they have already begun to explore prior to school.

Reading is but one sign system. As a sign system, it is a tool for change. Reading researchers today are not so interested in what a person takes away after reading a text but in how the reader has grown or changed by having had a reading experience. The key question a good reader ought to ask on completing a selection is not "What facts do I now know?" but rather "How have I changed as a function of having read?"

Conclusion

It is important, then, how researchers, teachers, parents, school board members, and administrators perceive reading. When viewed as a skill,

Figure 6. The uninterrupted writing of Megan, age four, shows the various signs by which she explores her identity.

reading is seen as a rote, rather mindless activity which needs to be practiced frequently in order to be maintained. When viewed as a tool for learning, reading is seen as a vehicle for critical thinking and growth. High-quality reading experiences, rather than the quantity of experiences, become important. The issue is not how many books children have read but what mental trips they have taken as a function of having read.

School policies ought thus to reflect what we currently know and understand about the reading process. Instructional policies should encourage teachers to set up functional reading and writing environments, to introduce and explore a variety of print settings, and actively to encourage children to use reading and writing to learn. Policymakers should be mindful that there are many different instructional methods and approaches available to reach these goals. School policy should set directions but not dictate materials and approaches. Teachers and researchers should be free to test their strongest instructional hypotheses for creating a supportive learning environment in their classrooms.

While some teachers and researchers might use learning centers as their organizational device, others might use a unit approach, and still others might use literature groups, science clubs, and self-selected units of study (see Harste, Short, and Burke 1988). We have been in classrooms where all these and other organizational devices have been successfully employed by teachers and researchers with the goal of improved reading instruction.

Supporting Self-Evaluation

Curriculum is a transaction between a plan of operation (a paper curriculum) and the mental trip that is taken by the language learner (the actualized curriculum). The relationship between these two aspects of curriculum is always dynamic, with each affecting the other. In order to develop a sound policy relative to evaluation, it is important to have a clear notion of what curriculum is and what it is not. In far too many of the classrooms we observed, curriculum was defined as the set of materials that was purchased for teachers and students to use. While materials are an important component of curriculum, to equate the two is to lose the one thing that curriculum should always offer — perspective.

In far too many other classrooms we observed, standardized tests became the curriculum. Scores on these tests determined what would be taught and in what order skills would be presented.

One of the most interesting findings of our review of recent research was how infrequently standardized tests of reading achievement are used as the criterion measure in studies of reading comprehension instruction. In fact, less than 5 percent of the studies we examined used standardized tests of reading comprehension. Most — 95 percent — contained researcher-designed tests or used other criteria (see Rowe 1985b). Schools, on the other hand, use standardized tests of reading achievement almost exclusively to document reading achievement and growth. In some districts we studied, administering standardized testing consumed fully one-ninth of the school year. In these same districts, instructional objectives were directly derived from the results of this testing and instructional activities were planned to correspond directly to particular subscores. Teachers were required to record the exact date that they began working on a particular skill, as well as any progress made and the date that mastery supposedly occurred.

The differences between school and research practice are in this instance striking. If we assume that researchers feel they are studying key cognitive operations in reading, then their behavior seems to say that standardized tests of reading do not measure these operations. Some researchers, in fact, have stated this quite plainly. Others say they do not know what standardized tests of reading measure (Langer and Pradl 1984).[31]

Defining "Test"

From an instructional standpoint, a test is any situation that affords educators the opportunity to make a decision that might improve instruction (Farr and Wolf 1984). This definition has two important implications. The first has to do with the relationship between labeling and curriculum; the second, with the need to expand the kinds of criterion measures used to judge effective reading.

First, defining a test as any situation that affords the opportunity for an improved instructional decision means that if tests are used simply to label children, they are being misused. From our observations misuse is widespread and is getting worse each year. In some districts a whopping 7-1/2 percent of the total school population was identified as needing "special education," and this figure was growing at a rate of one-half of a percent each year. Special-service units in some cooperatives are larger than entire school districts. In other districts students take a competency test at the end of their senior year and are labeled "competent" or "incompetent" upon graduation. Those labeled incompetent are offered no instructional program; they are just labeled and sent on their way.

These trends would be frightening even if standardized tests of reading were valid measures. The trends also indicate that the curriculum in regular education is failing and that, rather than our rethinking what is or should be happening, all sorts of children are being shunted off to special education. Further, reading is being used as the principal criterion for making these decisions.

On paper, special education has elaborate criteria designed to stop programs from becoming dumping grounds for the failures of regular education. Yet these safeguards fail, largely because if school systems give enough tests — especially tests that look less and less like real reading and more and more like tests of reading skills — they will always get the test data needed to support the claim that children are not doing well in the regular program (Goodman 1983, 1984). To find a disability, all one has to do is give enough tests. If enough are given, sooner or later some section on some test will be failed.

The second issue raised by our definition of a test concerns the criterion measures used to judge the success of a reading program.

Standardized tests are but one kind of criterion. They are not particularly good criteria if we take researchers and the critics of testing seriously. Teacher-made tests, informal observation, library usage, and ongoing performance on projects involving reading and writing are other kinds of criteria.

This criticism of standardized testing strongly suggests that a good program of evaluation needs to be multidimensional and reflective of the entire program, not of just its skills aspects.[32] Presently, if more than one measure of reading achievement is being used, the second measure is often another standardized test. Since these tests measure largely the same skills and are similar in theoretical orientation, the results tend to confirm each other rather than give a new perspective on the program. Students are put in double jeopardy. It is much like being tried twice for the same crime by the same judge and jury.

Although statewide testing is increasing in popularity, this is hardly the answer. Any educator who is really familiar with the state can predict, before the new test is developed, which districts, which schools, and which groups of children will come in first, second, and last. Standardized tests tend to prioritize the same things. Another test emphasizing the same old things won't solve anything. Alternate tests increase the likelihood that new voices will be heard and valued.

The current state of testing and the kinds of tests that are on the market make it especially important that multiple measures — formal as well as informal — be taken and used. These assessments need not be time-consuming or disruptive but can instead be made a part of the ongoing program of activity in the classroom.

Teachers can take the lead from researchers in this regard. In the studies we reviewed (see, for example, Siegel 1983, Rosen 1985, Wells 1985), testing embraced everything from art ("Draw a picture of what the story meant to you") to writing ("Now that we have read several fairy tales, test your understanding of fairy tales by writing one") to developing stories ("Now that we have read about Indiana in the early days, I'd like you to work with a neighbor and write a story showing what life was like from the perspective of someone who lived during this time").

Researchers have found that the best language testing situation is often a group of students working together — not a single student working in isolation.[33] Under group conditions a teacher can observe whether the learner takes advantage of the available social resources. Social skills are particularly important in the evaluation of language, since both reading and writing are social by their very nature. Writers, for example, rarely write alone and in silence. Most write, read, revise, permit others to read drafts, get feedback, revise, reread, and ask someone to edit — all before they send their work off to a publisher.

Skilled readers use what they have learned from discussions they have had while reading a book. They criticize, develop counterpoints, and essentially argue their way through books (see Harste 1988, Smith 1982, Sternglass and Smith 1984). Critical reading, like writing, is in this sense social. The strategies that good readers use are learned socially. What looks like a silent, private act has its foundations in social interaction. Teachers can create classroom environments which make the social resources of successful written language learning and use available to children. In such an environment, teachers can make ongoing observations of who uses which resources under what conditions. This is important information, not only for assessing the growth of the students in the room but for developing and redeveloping curriculum.

A Model of Curriculum

Evaluation ought not be something laid upon curriculum but rather an integral part of the curricular process. The districts we observed that used the results of the tests they administered to plan instruction were, in this sense, acting reasonably. Their error was in assuming that standardized tests could measure the things that were most significant in their program.

These points are clarified in Figure 7, which shows a schematized model of curriculum (adapted from Goodman, Burke, and Sherman 1980). Its key components are theory, evaluation, and instruction. Figure 7 suggests that we begin to plan a balanced reading curriculum based on four areas of knowledge: (1) our understanding of the reading process, (2) our understanding of the writing process, (3) our understanding of successful learners and users of written language, and (4) our understanding of the evolution of literacy. With this knowledge base established, curriculum planning can begin. Theoretical positions on each of these topics are available in public documents and need to be explicit and available for parents, teachers, and others to examine and revise as needed. The Edmonton Public Schools' position statement on reading and language arts is an example worth reading, as it reflects and incorporates more of our knowledge base than do most such documents.[34]

Evaluation, by this model, is (or ought to be) theoretically consistent with the underlying tenets of the balanced program outlined by the school district. The essential question evaluation asks is "In light of

THEORY

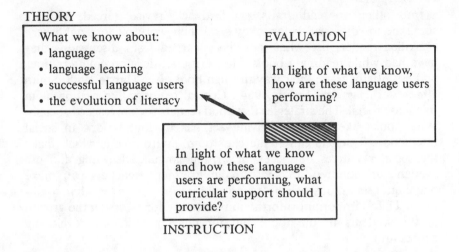

Figure 7. In this model of curriculum, there is a dynamic relationship between theory, instruction, and evaluation.

what we know about reading, writing, successful written language learning and use, and the evolution of literacy, how are these learners doing?" Notice that the question implies a social setting as well as observation of the learners in light of what we currently know. There is, in that sense, a conscious attempt to gather data that relate to our knowledge base and that allow for more intelligent decision making and instructional improvement.

Instruction, the third component of this model of curriculum, asks the question "In light of what we know, and of how well these language learners and users are doing, what instructional support should I provide?" Notice that this model suggests that instruction can be theoretically based and future-oriented. Instructional support can take many forms. New opportunities to test hypotheses in a low-risk environment are supportive. So is an instructional environment rich with opportunities and invitations to expand one's repertoire of reading and writing strategies.

Choice is an integral part of support. When the language user is allowed to choose whether to read the book on bridges or the book on badgers, he or she must make decisions and weigh pros and cons. Decision making, or choice, is what allows the language arts curriculum to operate offstage; it is what spurs students to read prior to reading, and to write when they are not assigned to write.

Evaluation, in this model, is an integral part of the instructional cycle. Its function is twofold: to inform theory and to inform instructional decision making. If evaluation does not serve these functions, it has no positive role to play in education.

Conclusion

In the final analysis, the goal of education is to create self-monitoring and self-evaluating learners. Administrators and school board members might take the lead by suggesting to teachers that it is their duty to demonstrate that they have a good language arts program, and that the program is getting better each year. Teachers, by the same token, can ask students to devise ways to demonstrate that they have indeed taken the mental trips that were planned and from which they were to have learned. Such a policy would not only improve evaluation but would be supportive of curriculum and curriculum development.

Many teachers welcome parents, administrators, and school board members into their classrooms. Visitors have an opportunity to discover which definition of reading is being played out in the classroom and to see reading from the perspective of the teacher and the pupils. Visitors should participate in planned activities, not just sit back and watch. Such participation increases the likelihood that the observer will experience the curriculum on a firsthand basis, through the eyes and from the perspective of a learner, instead of focusing on superficial features that might be unrelated to the actual curriculum that is occurring.

This kind of evaluation is much richer than attempting to make decisions about the quality of instruction based on the results of standardized tests. Most teachers are willing to share what they are using as criteria for deciding the value of their instructional activities. Not only should administrators and school board members ask teachers what their criteria are — they have a responsibility to do so.

The bottom line on evaluation, then, is that standardized tests do little to move teachers and pupils toward the goal of being self-monitoring learners, and they tell us little about the quality of a good language arts curriculum. If the currently available standardized tests cannot be used by teachers to make specific decisions to improve instruction, they should be abandoned.

Given a student with a score of 57 on the vocabulary subsection of a standardized test, I, for one, do not know what to teach. Given the opportunity to listen to a child read his or her favorite section of a self-selected library book, I can begin to note what strategies the student is and is not using.[35] Given the opportunity to sit in on two children discussing their reading, I can begin to note the kind and level of thinking they are engaging in. From this information, I can easily plan instruction. This is why, I suppose, researchers tend to avoid standardized tests and use in their place very direct measures of the behaviors, attitudes, and strategies that they associate with successful written language learning and use. In this instance, teachers, curriculum developers, administrators, and school board members can improve evaluation by taking the lead from researchers.

Effective Change Projects

In an attempt to determine what constitutes effective school change, we identified and studied school reading programs that exemplified dynamic, research-based instruction.[36] The programs that we focused on were developed in Arizona,[37] Colorado,[38] Hawaii,[39] Illinois,[40] Indiana,[41] Michigan,[42] Missouri,[43] New Hampshire,[44] New Mexico,[45] New York,[46] North Dakota,[47] Ohio,[48] Texas,[49] Edmonton,[50] Halifax,[51] and Winnipeg.[52] Several characteristics distinguished these programs:

Collaboration, Demonstration Centers, and Teacher Support Groups

First and almost inevitably, teachers and researchers worked collaboratively to effect school change. In the most effective programs a real partnership was developed. More often than not, classroom demonstration centers were created, and other teachers from the district and across the nation could and did visit these sites to understand what was going on. Often these teachers would take ideas home and try them in their own classrooms.

In one district the school board supported a two-week sabbatical program for teachers to spend time in the demonstration center classrooms. The visiting teachers spent two weeks in the demonstration classroom, actually working with the teacher. They received no money directly; instead, the sabbatical paid for a substitute teacher for their classes.

This collaboration process often resulted in a network of teachers who met regularly to study and share what they were doing and to gather ideas about what to do next. Sometimes the groups met monthly, sometimes only in the summer. Some formed study groups and continued to meet regularly throughout the year. These networks were in a sense teacher support groups.

More often than not, successful support groups had an academic leader from a local university. While university personnel often provided a focus, the exciting dimension of these programs was that teachers were helping teachers. They not only shared articles that they had found but formed work groups with shared common values and experiences.

Over and over again teachers who were involved in projects of this sort were active in professional organizations. Many teacher support groups ran inservice programs for the district, taught workshops, and were frequent presenters at state and national meetings of reading and language arts educators. Many of the teachers in these projects had decided to do advanced study in reading, writing, or the language arts. Professionally, these attitudes and experiences put them well ahead of their less active colleagues.

Teaching as Inquiry

The single feature that most characterized these programs was the teachers' attitude about learning in general, not about any particular activity. In fact, the activities ranged from groups of teachers working on how to improve reading comprehension, to other groups principally focused on writing, to still others interested in exploring how reading and writing might be more successfully integrated in the classroom. Some focused on regular education, others on special education or bilingual problems, and still others on inner-city concerns.

These groups set out to build viable instructional programs based on recent insights into and understanding of the reading process. Teachers took risks, discussed options, tried them out, and then rehashed them in terms of what had happened and how the activities might be improved. During teacher support group meetings, other teachers were invited and often took these ideas back to their classrooms, trying them out there and discussing differences, achievements, and possible revisions or extensions. Teachers in these programs were real learners. They were in pursuit of a practical theory of literacy. In visiting several of these groups, we found an excitement about teaching, children, and learning that was refreshing to see in these days of talk about teacher burnout and school failure.

Theoretically Based Programs

Unlike demonstration centers in the past, in which there was an attempt to disseminate programs that work regardless of their base in theory, teachers in these programs had a firm grip on theory. The longer their involvement, the more firmly grounded they seemed to become.

There were no general patterns of where the groups began, though the one pattern that seemed to emerge was that issues of immediate and practical concern were often addressed first. It was only later that theoretical consistency and larger issues were addressed.

In these groups, change started small and grew as new aspects of the curriculum were brought into focus and discussed. Rarely was change associated with the selection of a new reading series, the use of a new standardized test of reading, or the introduction of a new management system. More frequently, change began with a particular classroom project (for example, creating a library for the children to use) or specific lessons which the teacher was planning to present (Stephens 1986).

In studies which focused on integrating reading and writing, the teacher and researcher often exchanged roles. Lessons were videotaped as they were taught. Afterwards both the teacher and researcher watched the videotape and wrote a narrative on what they viewed as the most significant thing that happened. These narratives were compared and formed the basis of discussion, clarification, and improved instruction.

Teachers often modified theory and practice in interesting ways. In all the programs we visited, teachers knew how to talk about what they were doing or attempting to do in their classrooms. With time, theory and practice came to be used as self-correction devices for each other. Practices that were no longer theoretically consistent with the position teachers had come to hold were reexamined and revised to be theoretically consistent with the rest of the program. In like fashion, theories were revised and strengthened based on practice.

Leadership and Change

Intellectual leadership came from many sources. In some instances, it was the principal. By and large, principals who were effective change agents administered more by wandering than by fiat. Rarely were they in their office. Most spent up to 70 percent of their time in classrooms, working with and learning with teachers. Few acted as if they had the answers; rather, their approach was "Let's try it and see." (This is not to suggest that effective change agents were eclectic in their approach to reading. All took strong positions, knew what they wanted, and worked to support teachers and the changes they were attempting to make.)

Principals, however, were not the key agents of change in many schools or districts that had successful programs. When they were, school change seemed to go smoothly. Some weak principals were effective largely because they knew enough to turn leadership over to a subordinate or to a knowledgeable professional at a neighboring college.

In all cases effective change programs seemed to be associated with particular people. In each case, some one person or a group of people took leadership. Sometimes this was a classroom teacher who was perceived as knowing a lot about reading; sometimes it was the reading specialist; sometimes it was a curriculum supervisor; and sometimes it was someone from a local college or university.

Effective change agents began by working with one person in one classroom instead of with all of the teachers in the building. Successes in this room were shared with other interested teachers. Schoolwide change seemed to occur rapidly, once a critical mass — about 60 percent or more — of the teachers had moved in a certain direction.

What was surprising to us was how often principals and administrators were seen as obstacles to progress in what were, in our estimation, very effective change projects. Repeatedly, school policy seemed geared to support the weakest teachers in the district rather than the strongest. Teachers in many projects complained that they were often asked to implement practices and sit through inservice programs that violated what they knew about language, language learning, and good teaching. Policies such as these are extremely shortsighted. One administrator told me that creative teachers in his district did not need to follow the restrictive management plan that several teachers had complained to me about. When I asked him what a teacher would have to do to be seen as "creative," however, he could not answer.

Of course, this is a real problem both for the principal and the teacher, to say nothing about the teaching profession and the future. There are no simple answers to the issues raised here. But too often, in dealing with perplexing situations, we forget that we have gained significant knowledge about teaching and learning and can put that knowledge to use. Teaching and learning involve a human relationship. It takes two willing participants to engage in the process. As a teacher, I create a supportive language-learning environment based on what I know, and I invite children to participate and to take the mental trips that I associate with successful language learning and use. As an administrator, I can only do the same.

Teacher Choice

Change was rarely forced upon teachers in the most effective school projects. Rather, teachers were provided the opportunity and the support to test ideas they felt were consistent with the direction they sought to take. Mandated school change rarely worked. Change agents often began by working with teachers who were the most amenable to change rather than by taking on the teachers most resistant to change. In some instances change began with only one teacher; in big districts, such as the Denver Public Schools, the number was as large as 125. Typically, when the number was large a select group of teachers (twelve, in the case of Denver) was identified and worked with intensely. Teachers who were not ready to change or who felt strongly about what they were currently doing in the classroom were permitted to continue their own programs. All teachers were invited to take as small or as large steps as they liked. Small steps typically led to bigger steps and bigger change.

Most of these programs involved much more complex and elaborate changes than did the typical research study we reviewed as part of this project. Modest hypotheses grew into exciting and multifaceted programs of reading, writing, and learning. Rarely were timid hypotheses being tested.

On the whole nothing achieves like success. While personnel in these projects often talked about the need to get to administrators, other teachers, school board members, state department of education people, federal policymakers, and others, in the end it was their own experience and classrooms that did the most to sell the programs to themselves, other teachers, and district administrators. Teachers often initially worried about doing the program right. With time, they realized that this was the wrong attitude; that essentially, they had only to begin. They, like the children in their classrooms, had the right to make mistakes and grow from them.

Parent Involvement

Parent involvement was central to the success of many programs (see Steffel 1985, Hill 1980). Parents often acted in support of teachers and defended the program when administrators seemed unsupportive.

In the most successful programs there was a conscious effort to keep parents informed. No single format for parent involvement was prevalent; parents generally were provided options as to how they might participate.

Most programs had parents' nights of some sort. The most successful parent programs seemed to be those in which the children were in charge of planning. In these instances, teachers used some time during parents' night to present their program and discuss it with parents.

Effective programs tended to treat parents as partners in learning. Classrooms were open to parents, and parents were invited to participate rather than just to watch.

Parent education was an important component of inservice. Teachers took the attitude that parents had a right to be informed, that it was in the profession's interest to do so, and that parents will ask for programs that reflect what they know. If we want parents to be supportive of change, then it is in our interest to support their learning.

Time

Effective programs of change occurred only over time. There were no quick fixes. Extended involvement by a core group of people seemed to be a key factor. Often experts from outside the district were brought in, but these visits were well-chosen and carefully timed.

In some instances experts really said nothing new. Their role appeared to be to legitimize the direction in which the local group was attempting to move. On the average, programs of change had been in place from three to seven years, with many extended beyond this. In some cases programs had grown from a few teachers to encompass the building or the district. In no case was change a one-shot event. Real change occurred only over long periods of time and where real feelings of trust and ownership of the program had been shared and developed, especially among collaborating teachers and researchers.

The Agenda Ahead

This document was written to help teachers, researchers, curriculum developers, administrators, and school board members establish public school policy on the teaching of reading. As a consequence of the explosion of knowledge in the field of reading during the past ten years, language educators know more about reading processes than ever before. It is crucial to the future of reading and teaching that educators be given the opportunity to build reflexively on this knowledge base. To recommend that educators improve school reading programs by returning to the basics is equivalent to recommending that the medical profession abandon everything it has learned and return to bloodletting.[53]

School and instructional policies which focus on the weakest students and teachers rather than the strongest students and teachers are short-sighted. Just as instructional programs which fail to let students test their best language hypotheses are misguided, so are district policies which fail to let teachers test their best hypotheses. Because of entrenched policies and practices, there are some schools and districts where neither teachers nor students can learn. This, it seems to me, is the most devastating statement that can be made about the state of public education in our society.

As new policies are established, it is important to remember that the process by which the best teachers, researchers, and students grow is the very process which the poorest learners must engage in if they too are to grow. While the specific details vary, there is but one learning process.

Poor kids learn in the same way as rich kids. Our best research evidence suggests that most regular education students learn in the same way as most special education students, and vice versa. This finding must be kept in mind when considering a policy favoring children coming from certain kinds of homes but recommending a different, often more structured program for students labeled poor or culturally disadvantaged or special (Stephens 1986). It follows that any environment structured so as to be conducive to our own learning will also, according to the available evidence, be the environment most

47

conducive to the learning of others, despite their labels. Intellectual welfare systems serve no one.[54]

This report calls for a collaborative pedagogy, a pedagogy in which educators in colleges and educators in elementary and secondary schools work together. What we need is basic educational research grounded in the current knowledge base but focused toward the development of a practical theory of literacy instruction.

Basic reading research in education is different from basic reading research in psychology, sociology, or linguistics. Researchers in those disciplines can decide to study social interaction and nothing more. Some may even decide to limit their investigations to only certain aspects of the reading process, such as how the graphophonemic system works or what happens during the period when the eyes are on the page.

Educators do not have this luxury. Educators must act come Monday morning. In addition to knowing reading theory, they must know writing theory, learning theory, child growth and development, curriculum theory, and more. The business of education is synthesis. The role of the educator is that of synthesizer, whether the educator is in the university or the public elementary school. Because the business of education is synthesis and use, basic educational research is more complex than other types of research.

Certainly we benefit from better explanations of the basic operations in language and learning. But these findings still must be interpreted and tested by basic educational research if they are to result in an improved theory of literacy instruction and improved educational practice. To accomplish this, teaching must be viewed as inquiry and researching as teaching. Intellectual leadership for a new theory of literacy instruction will benefit from school and university collaboration as well as from a wider participation and involvement of all educators in basic educational research.

Learning entails one part activity to one part reflexivity. The policy guidelines which follow attempt to capture the activity — what is currently going on in the best of sites — as well as the reflexivity — what teachers, researchers, curriculum developers, administrators, and school board members ought to be doing to make connections between research and practice.

Guidelines for Improving Reading Comprehension Instruction

The following guidelines encapsulate available information about the conditions that are likely to improve the teaching of reading in our schools. These guidelines are written to help educators evaluate current school policies and practices and to formulate new ones. They build on what we have learned about reading from both research and practice, and are designed to move teachers, researchers, curriculum developers, and administrators beyond risk — toward creating communities of language learners.

1. *Teachers should plan a reading curriculum which is broad enough to accommodate every student's growth, flexible enough to adapt to individual and cultural characteristics of pupils, specific enough to assure growth in language and thinking, and supportive enough to guarantee student success.* Research shows that children in even supposedly homogeneous reading groups differ greatly from one another. Thus, curricular experiences selected for reading instruction should be open-ended, allowing each student to participate regardless of previous experience or school level. Individual or group research projects, learner-centered literature study groups, and pen-pal letter exchange programs are three examples of open-ended activities which allow students to take risks, to test their latest language hypotheses, and to proceed at their own rate. To improve the status of literacy in our society, it is crucial that populations not currently well-served be better served and that all students achieve to their potential. Curriculum failure on this guideline is indicated when disproportionate numbers of boys or minority students are not succeeding or when there is a general increase in the number of children being labeled "in need of special education."

2. *Effective teachers of reading create classroom environments in which children actively use reading and writing as tools for learning.* Research shows that children tend to use learning strategies in the manner in which the strategies have been taught. Teachers can demonstrate the usefulness of reading and writing by offering opportunities for children to engage in meaningful reading and writing during content-area instruction. Library research projects, the integration of reading

and writing in the content areas, and classroom activities that engage students in reading and writing in the ways they are used outside of school meet this guideline. Reading and writing taught as isolated subjects violate this guideline.

3. *Good language arts programs highlight reading and writing but actively encourage students to use speech, art, music, drama, and dance in their attempts to communicate and grow.* Reader's theater, art projects, plays, dioramas, and songwriting should be integral parts of the reading program. Not only should teachers provide opportunities for these experiences, but they should take time to discuss with the children how such activities highlight, add to, or even change text interpretation and appreciation. Classroom projects and student presentations involving a variety of media are signs that this guideline is being met.

4. *Teachers should set up functional reading and writing environments.* Children learn to read by reading and learn to write by writing. Teachers should invite children daily to read and write, and should provide uninterrupted time for them to do so. Message boards, journals, learning logs, news reports, book sales, and writing out of daily plans are but some of the techniques used by effective teachers of reading. Teacher-selected rather than student-selected topics for reading and writing violate this guideline, as do curricular fragmentation and teaching content-area subjects in ways that let students avoid rather than actively engage in reading. Reading and writing activities that have no intrinsic value — that is, that serve no function other than to provide seatwork — also violate this guideline.

5. *Teachers should encourage children to utilize their higher-level cognitive abilities by systematically planning instructional experiences which introduce and invite children to try a variety of reading comprehension strategies such as storying, visualizing, inferencing, summarizing, and generalizing, as well as drawing conclusions based on intuition, the information in the text, and logic. In addition children should routinely be encouraged to relate what they already know to what they are reading.* This means that teachers will spend less time having children complete workbooks and skill sheets and allow more time for children actively to use and apply their growing understandings. Literature groups in which children choose and critically talk about and defend their interpretation of the books they have read are but one instructional technique which teachers might employ in creatively meeting this guideline. This guideline is violated when instruction is differentiated into groups in which some students do vocabulary study or are asked only literal-level questions and are not given the opportunity to think as other students are encouraged to think.

6. *Choice is an integral part of the literacy process.* Children should be permitted to choose reading materials, activities, and ways of demonstrating their understanding of the texts they have read. Reading skills and strategies should be presented as options rather than as rules to be universally applied under all reading conditions. Teachers should issue invitations to read and write rather than make reading and writing assignments. Teacher-directed instruction in which all children in a classroom or reading group are required to make the same response indicates that this guideline is not being met.

7. *Beginning reading instruction should provide children with many opportunities to interact in meaningful print contexts: listening to stories, participating in shared book experiences, making language-experience stories and books, composing stories through play, enacting stories through drama, and reading and writing predictable books.* If children do not have extensive book experiences prior to coming to school, teachers must begin by reading to them and by providing them with the reading experiences they have missed. Good beginning reading programs do not assume that some children have not had meaningful encounters with print but rather build from as well as extend what children already know about language. From the first day of school, books and paper and pens should be in the hands of children instead of the teacher. Whole-class workbook readiness activities, kindergarten and first-grade classrooms in which children are seated at desks analyzing rather than using language, plans to move the first-grade curriculum to kindergarten, and high numbers of students being retained in kindergarten and first grade due to poor readiness scores are indicators that current school policies and practices need reexamination.

8. *Research shows that children learn language best in a low-risk environment in which they are permitted and encouraged to test hypotheses of interest to them.* Experiences should be planned which allow children to take risks, make inferences, check their conclusions against the evidence at hand, and be wrong. Reading teachers should help children understand that predicting what will happen next in stories, jumping to conclusions, and confirming or disconfirming their hypotheses are effective and powerful reading strategies rather than errors. For the most part, teachers should avoid questions that suggest right answers and instead ask questions that encourage a diversity of well-supported responses. Penalties for being wrong, as well as an overemphasis on correctness, grades, and being right by either students or teachers are indications that this guideline is not being met.

9. *Effective teachers of reading understand that growth in literacy is marked by plateaus and peaks over time.* When reading and writing

are used as tools for learning, first-draft efforts must be treated with respect and students not made to feel vulnerable. Teachers must value the future as well as the present and provide supportive opportunities for children to revisit promising first drafts and then move to some more final form. First-draft reading and writing assignments handed in by children under strict time deadlines, on-the-spot corrections of oral reading miscues, and other teacher monitoring techniques which give students dysfunctional views of what it means to be a successful reader or writer violate this guideline.

10. *Reading instruction should include a wide variety of materials and reading experiences.* Teachers should maintain and use, as an integral part of the reading program at all grade levels, a well-stocked classroom library which includes poetry, newspapers, and trade books as well as content-area books and magazines. Fiction and nonfiction materials should be selected on the basis of quality and student interest and should represent a wide range of difficulty. Content-area teachers should use multiple textbooks and trade books, and set up environments in which students work on self-selected topics within the units of study addressed at each grade level in their discipline. Children in all classrooms should have free and unlimited access to print materials. Student desks containing a variety of books, student folders which include a range of writing from poetry to research reports, and diverse student projects and presentations indicate that this guideline is being met.

11. *Teachers should provide daily opportunities for children to share and discuss what they have been reading and writing.* As part of this sharing time, the teacher should help children to value the reading strategies they already have, and also continually introduce and invite children to try new ones. Research reveals that both learning and language are social events. To this end, teachers and administrators should celebrate writings of their own, of others, and of their students. In addition, they should read widely, write and read when their students write and read, and actively share the strategies they are using to solve literacy problems that interest them. Author sharing times, peer tutoring activities, and collaborative student research projects are but a few of the activities that teachers might institute in meeting this objective in their classrooms.

12. *Teachers should understand that how they teach is just as important as what they teach.* This means that skills should be introduced as options that readers have when encountering unknown items in print, and that children should be taught that deciding which strategy to use

under each condition is an integral part of what it means to be a strategic reader. To this end, good teachers of reading and writing encourage risk taking in an effort to help children understand and value the linguistic resources they have at their own disposal. They provide demonstrations by reading and writing with their students. Children who wait in line for the teacher to answer a question prior to proceeding, who are unwilling to take risks when reading or writing, and who exhibit misconceptions about how to successfully use reading and writing are indications that mixed curricular messages are being given.

13. *Effective programs of evaluation are multidimensional and define testing broadly as any situation that affords the opportunity to make an improved instructional decision.* In lieu of, or in addition to, standardized tests, effective evaluators directly observe important behaviors, attitudes, and strategies that they associate with successful written language use, learning, and teaching. Program decisions for students in the areas of placement (gifted and talented or special education) and promotion (whether in terms of readiness to read in first grade or graduation from high school in twelfth grade) that are based on single test measures or that weigh standardized test results over other data (teacher, parent, or student judgment; classroom performance reports; etc.) violate this guideline. Similarly, advancement policies in reading that are based on test performance alone, even when the test was specifically designed for the materials used, must be questioned.

14. *Effective programs of evaluation in reading focus on curriculum and encourage teachers and pupils to engage reflexively in self-evaluation as they use each other as curricular informants.* Effective administrators do not mandate evaluation criteria but rather ask teachers to assume this professional responsibility and give them the freedom to do so in creative ways. Effective teachers, by the same token, provide children options as to how they will demonstrate that they have grown as a result of their engagement in an experience involving reading. Merit pay attached to standardized achievement test results is a blatant violation of this guideline, as are tracking and grouping practices which fail to provide some students with as rich a learning environment as other students.

15. *Effective administrators and school board members recognize teachers as learners and support their professional right to try to improve the status of literacy instruction.* They do so by actively encouraging teachers to test their best hypotheses about what constitutes effective

literacy instruction. Teachers should be provided with inservice training and time off to attend professional meetings. Professional self-development can be fostered through the creation and encouragement of teacher support groups. High rates of teacher burnout suggest that teachers have not been able to maintain key professional rights and responsibilities.

16. *Effective administrators and school boards see teachers as key resources for the revitalization of education.* Effective administrators use teachers as curricular informants, respect teachers as capable and professional decision makers, and confirm and legitimize teacher intuition. Lack of teacher requests to try innovative techniques and approaches to the teaching of reading, the presence of "teacher-proof" materials, and central-office skill check-off lists are but some indications that this guideline needs to be addressed.

17. *Effective school policy on reading and language arts sets directions but does not dictate which materials and programs will be used to teach reading.* Effective school administrators organize districtwide curriculum committees and provide other forums for teacher input on what materials will be purchased and used. Research indicates that often the most effective materials are those purposely constructed or selected by the researcher or teacher for specific purposes and specific children. Good teachers plan a variety of activities which engage students and are geared to their needs and interests. Districtwide dictates and central-office skill check-off lists based on particular reading series or tests suggest that this policy guideline is being violated. High utilization of school resource materials centers, budgets for teachers to order materials specifically for their classroom, and the active involvement of teachers as collaborators in what materials are to be available in the school indicate that this guideline is being met.

18. *Effective programs of reading treat parents as participants and partners in learning who are permitted options, choices, involvement, and information about the instructional alternatives available to students.* Parents of children who become successful readers are active in their child's education. It is recommended that every teacher schedule a parents' day in which the goals, objectives, methods, and rationale being used to teach reading are fully explained to parents. Parent conferences should begin with the probe "What do you know about your child that would help me be a better teacher this year?" Frequent parent requests that their child be placed with specific teachers, parent involvement in classrooms (typing student manuscripts, making blank books, etc.), and high parent attendance at school functions are signs that this guideline is being met.

19. *Effective programs of change work under the assumption that curriculum and curriculum development take time and are enhanced by partnership.* Such programs facilitate and encourage collaboration between educators in college and educators in classrooms as they actively engage in the pursuit of practical theory. Effective administrators take every opportunity to encourage teacher, student, parent, and university collaboration. Joint school and university research projects that extend over time, and community programs such as Literacy Day, Reading at the Mall, Young Authors Conference, and the like, are signs that this guideline is being practiced. Town and gown splits, as well as poor relationships between the reading curriculum coordinator and reading faculty at the local college or university, are signs that existing policies and practices need to be reexamined.

20. *Teachers, students, parents, administrators, university personnel, and school board members should do everything possible to portray themselves as a supportive and active community of language learners.* They do this by using reading to learn about reading and by collaboratively building policies about reading that highlight and promote learning and growth.

Notes

1. In October 1983, Indiana University received a federal contract to do research on reading comprehension with special education students. The first year was devoted to reviewing the literature. We began by reading reviews of reading comprehension research and then used these reviews to generate a list of topics of interest to the field (schemata, inferencing, story structure, etc.). This list was used to develop a tentative taxonomy for coding research studies. Next, we began a three-pronged attack: locating relevant studies from 1974–84, coding the studies, and revising the taxonomy as needed. A detailed discussion of our methodology and findings is reported in Crismore 1985 (available through the ERIC system — ED 261 350).

During the second year, our task was to observe classroom practice. We were to gather information about the teaching of reading comprehension in nine districts or school cooperatives. Advanced Technology Incorporated (ATI), an independent research corporation, was subcontracted to design the case-study plan, identify appropriate sites, and train research personnel. This plan was submitted to a national advisory panel consisting of experts in reading, research, writing, and special education. This panel recommended that we focus our research on what was happening in classrooms identified as exemplary by the administrator in each district. Their rationale was that the profession had little to learn from watching bad instruction. Since the intent of the project was to improve the teaching of reading comprehension, the panel further recommended that we adopt an ethnographic perspective and approach our task with the assumption that a theory of reading comprehension was operating in each classroom. Our role as researchers, then, was to map that theory and determine what kept it in place.

The panel also recommended that we report the results of our observations as "thick classroom descriptions." Identification and interpretation of co-occurring patterns and anomalies within and across classrooms, as well as reflections on what might be done to improve instruction given the current state of knowledge, should occur later, once we had time to think about our on-site experiences. The panel suggested that rather than present what we found as "objective truth" we put ourselves "in the text" so that readers might hear from us as well as from the field. The rationale was that we had been contacted because of our expertise, and readers of our final report should have access to our detailed descriptions as well as be able to benefit from a synthesis of our work and thinking. Harste and Stephens 1985 is a detailed report of our findings and the procedures which we followed (available through the ERIC system — ED 264 544). We are also preparing another volume based on the final reports of the federally funded study. See Harste and Stephens, in process.

2. Mikulecky 1981 argues on the basis of his research studying literacy in the workplace that school-literacy tasks are quite different from job-literacy tasks. Harste and Mikulecky 1984 make a similar argument distinguishing early literacy learning from beginning reading and writing programs. In the area of writing, Odell 1980 argues that writing instruction is often quite different from real-world writing.

3. For a description of some of the characteristics of recent research in reading see Snyder 1985. For a discussion of the laboratory approach in language research in general, see Mischler 1979.

4. For a review of conceptual trends in reading comprehension research see Harste 1985b.

5. My impression is that the profession has moved from experimental research to ethnography in a search for a new research paradigm. More recently the shortcomings of an ethnographic paradigm have also been noted. The new paradigm which seems to be evolving is what I would call collaborative research. To trace this move see Edelsky 1984, Erickson 1984, Green and Bloome 1983, Mischler 1979, Carey 1980, Magoon 1977, Short 1986, Smith 1984, and Stephens 1985.

6. There is a growing group of research studies and projects that move in this direction. For a complete listing see Note 25.

7. See Notes 38 and 45.

8. One of these projects became the focus of a videotape series for use with preservice and inservice teacher education. See Harste and Jurewicz 1985.

9. See, for example, Anderson et al. 1985, Boyer 1984, Cash 1984, Goodlad 1984, and the National Commission on Excellence in Education 1983. See also Psacharopoulos 1981, Chall 1983, Eckland 1982, Harnischfeger and Wiley 1975, Kozol 1985, and Ravitch 1985.

Cross-cultural comparisons inevitably show that other countries educate better. International comparisons are difficult to interpret, as often only a small portion of the population is in school in these countries, yet this elite group is often compared to all students in the U.S. at a particular age. See, for example, Thorndike 1973 and Stevenson 1984.

10. This same phenomenon has been reported by others. See Barr 1974–75; DeLawter 1970; Franklin 1984; Harste 1980; Harste and Burke 1977; and Rhodes 1978, 1979.

11. For further explanation of these instructional strategies, see Buchanan 1980, Cochran et al. 1984, McCracken and McCracken 1979, Martin and Brogan 1971, Rhodes 1981, and Milz 1980.

12. While Jason's writing sample makes him appear developmentally further along than the writers in the phonics and skills classrooms, this phenomenon has been reported before and has been found not to be evidence of initial differences between groups. Kenneth Goodman, for example, has reported that under uninterrupted story reading conditions students who seemed unable to read suddenly struck teachers as being more capable. For reports on how a supportive context affects performance in reading and writing see Goodman 1965, Harste and Carey 1985, Jenkins 1980, and Stephens and Harste 1986.

13. This point is made by several researchers. See especially Rowe 1985a.

14. Although I define reading somewhat differently, this definition best reflects the dominant definition of reading among researchers today. See Harste 1985b.

15. These samples were collected in a junior high special education classroom in which the children had been taught strategies whereby they could support each other during the reading of complex text materials. Reading was very much a social event, with pairs of students often discussing what they had read paragraph by paragraph throughout a selection. Reading in this classroom was quite different from what it was in classrooms which maintained an individualized reading program. Too often "individualized instruction" has come to be operationalized as "isolated instruction" in classrooms. This is unfortunate. Open-entry and open-ended activities such as literature study and journal writing are individualized yet social (in the sense that children can share and thus learn from one another).

16. Rowe 1985a and 1985b are reviews of the research in reading metacognition. The primary sources include Anderson, Spiro, and Montague 1977; Bussie 1982; Brown 1977, 1981, 1982; Brown and Smiley 1977; van Dijk 1977, 1979; Gollasch 1982a, 1982b; Pearson 1984; Sherman 1979; Spiro, Bruce, and Brewer 1980; Winograd 1983; Winograd et al. 1984; and Winograd and Johnston 1982.

17. For how this concept relates to young children, see Baghban 1984; Bissex 1980; Harste, Woodward, and Burke 1984; Heath 1983; Jaggar and Smith-Burke 1985; Ferreiro and Teberosky 1982; Goodman and Goodman 1979; Meek 1982; Lindfors 1980; Taylor 1983; Teale 1978, 1982; Wells 1981; and Wells, Barnes, and Wells 1984.

18. See citations listed in Note 16. See also Downing 1970, 1979; Goodman, Burke, and Sherman 1980; Mattingly 1972, 1979; and Yaden and Templeton 1985.

19. Often 25 million is quoted as the number of illiterates in America. This number is a projected figure from a Texas study (Northcutt 1975) that asked successful middle-class Americans how they used reading and writing to function in their work and lives. Using what this sample gave as base responses, researchers sampled a larger population and judged them as to whether they used reading and writing in the same ways as the criterion group. Twenty-two million were projected as not being able to use reading and writing as the criterion group used reading and writing. Despite the theoretical problems with this study and the fact that it has been severely criticized by several scholars, it continues to be quoted. Roger Farr asked the federal government for a copy of the original report and maintains that there is not enough data presented to be able to make sense out of the study (personal communication). Tom Stitch argues that Jonathan Kozol's 60 million illiterate Americans, who are reading between the fifth- and eighth-grade levels, are not illiterate at all but rather "undereducated." This is a quite different problem and calls for a quite different solution than adult literacy programs which focus on phonics. See Farr and Fay 1982; Farr, Fay, and Negley 1978; Goodman 1983; and Stitch 1983, 1985.

20. For a list of studies, see Appendix B in Crismore 1985.

21. See Note 20.

22. See Note 20.

23. See Note 20.

24. Schema-theoretic approaches to reading essentially have much in common with psycholinguistic models. The following citations are considered classics, and firmly established a schema-theoretic perspective on reading: Adams and Collins 1978, Rumelhart 1977, Rumelhart and Ortony 1977, Spiro 1977.

25. There are currently several reading and writing curricular studies in progress at various curricular levels. Each of these studies entails extensive collaborative work with teachers in planning and implementing curriculum. See the following for work in preschool, kindergarten, and first grade: Clyde 1985, Pierce 1984, Short 1986.

For work at the elementary school level, see Calkins 1984; Harste and Jurewicz 1985; Hansen and Graves 1984; Tierney, Pearson, and Tucker 1984.

For work in special education see Stephens 1985.

Work at the college level for the most part involves the researcher serving simultaneously as researcher and teacher. For work at this level, see Bissex 1985, Brandt 1985, Dahl 1984, Kucer 1983.

26. M. A. K. Halliday initially developed this formulation in working with school personnel in Australia. His argument is that every instance of language use allows language users the opportunity to learn language, to learn about language, and to learn through language. He further argues that all three of these opportunities should be present in every classroom activity that teachers plan. See Christie 1980.

27. See the 1984 joint NCTE and IRA position paper criticizing readability formulas. Among other things it says,

"... research has shown that student interest in the subject-matter plays a significant role in determining the readability of materials. ...

"Matching students with textbooks at appropriate levels of difficulty, therefore, is a complex and difficult task. Various pressures have forced publishers to use readability formulae to assure purchasers that their textbooks are properly 'at grade level.' Unfortunately, these formulae measure only average sentence and word length to determine the difficulty of passages. Although long words and sentences sometimes create problems of comprehension, they do not always do so. For example, the sentence 'To be or not to be' is short, but it includes difficult concepts. This sentence, 'The boy has a big, red apple for lunch and some cookies for a snack,' is long but simple. Readability formulae would allow the first sentence but not the second. ...

"Serious problems occur when publishers use readability formulae. ... The language doesn't sound natural to the student. ... [C]omplex ideas, which depend on complex sentences, cannot be adequately written. ... [T]here is a real danger that makers of instructional materials will avoid using interesting and important works of literature because those works ... don't 'fit the formula.'

"Educators and publishers should use alternative approaches for measuring text difficulty. Procedures should include:

1. Teacher evaluation of proposed texts, based on the teacher's knowledge of their students' prior information and experiences ...

2. Teacher observations of students using proposed texts in instructional settings, in order to evaluate the effectiveness of the material.

3. Checklists for evaluating the readability of the proposed materials, involving attention to such variables as student interest, text graphics, the number and difficulty of ideas and concepts in the material, the length of lines in the text, and the many other factors which contribute to relative difficulty of text material." (p. 1)

For a free copy of the joint statement, send a self-addressed stamped envelope to: Readability, Membership Service Representative, NCTE, 1111 Kenyon Road, Urbana, IL 61801.

28. The International Reading Association, under the direction of Mark Aulls, currently is attempting to collect and publish a volume summarizing studies which explore reading and writing relationships.

29. The conceptualization in Figure 5 is adapted from the writing of John Murray (1984). The model was first published in Harste 1985a.

30. Reflexivity is defined by Michael Herzfeld as the active use of self in order to learn. See Herzfeld 1983.

31. In this document, Langer and Pradl report on a two-year research project which examined the strategies students use to comprehend and answer questions from selected norm-based standardized multiple-choice test items. Langer suggests caution in using the results of such tests to make decisions about any individual's performance or ability (see citation below). From her detailed interview procedures, she discovered that not only did students get the right answer for the wrong reason and vice versa, but that sometimes they never had the opportunity to demonstrate their understanding of the passage at all. Langer concludes that such tests "appear to have become a 'genre' unto themselves and, although successful performance on these items may in some way be related to comprehension ability, the tests themselves do not directly measure the processes involved in the development of reading comprehension nor do they evaluate an individual student's ability to manage the comprehension processes" (p. 765).
See also Farr and Carey 1986, Johnston 1983, Langer 1985, Neuraka 1982.

32. For an excellent discussion of the issues involved in testing as well as the direction in which the profession needs to move, see Eisner 1985 and Johnston 1987. See also Cousin 1985.

33. In the words of Vygotsky, "The zone of proximal development . . . is the distance between the actual developmental level as determined by independent problem solving and the level of potential development as described through problem solving under adult guidance or in collaboration with more capable peers. The actual developmental level characterizes mental development retrospectively, while the zone of proximal development characterizes mental development prospectively. . . . Thus, the notion of a zone of proximal development enables us to propound a new formula, namely, that the only 'good learning' is that which is in advance of development" (1978, pp. 86–87). See also Wertsch 1979.

34. Edmonton Public School District. 1982. *A Language Working Paper* (mimeo). Edmonton: L. A. Services, Edmonton Public School District. This statement was originally drafted by Dennis Searle when he was on leave from the University of Alberta and working in the Edmonton Public Schools with Margaret Stevenson, Supervisor of Language Arts. See Note 50.

35. Analysis of oral reading has had a long tradition in reading instruction. Although no one has really addressed the issue of what constitutes a "miscue" in a retelling, even an introduction to the procedures for analyzing oral reading miscues is useful in helping teachers reconceptualize reading from a psycholinguistic perspective and in developing a "mental set" for assessing reading growth and planning instruction. See Goodman et al. 1986 and Carey, in press.

36. In addition to the projects listed below, other projects by Nancie Atwell and Susan Stires (Boothbay Harbor, Maine), Donna Alverman (University of Georgia), Donna Ogle (National College of Education), Linda Crafton (Northeastern University, Evanston), Tim Perkins (Northeastern College, Boston), and others bear observation.

37. Carol Edelsky, Karen Smith, and Barbara Flores have been working in various Arizona schools and settings, such as Phoenix, Chandler, and Lincoln. They are attempting to apply collaboratively current insights in language and language learning to bilingual instruction. The teacher support group in the area is called SMILE and is one of the largest in the nation. Contact Carol Edelsky, Karen Smith, or Barbara Flores at Elementary Education, Arizona State University, Tempe, AZ 85281. Contact Ralph Peterson at the same address for SMILE. See Flores et al. 1985.

Yetta Goodman, Ken Goodman, Dorothy King, and Sena Fitzpatrick have been working together in the Navajo and Papago schools at Chinle, Wingate, and Gallup over an extended period in the area of reading comprehension. One of these efforts involved replicating Donald Graves's writing project on the Papago Reservation. Contact Yetta Goodman, University of Arizona, College of Education, Tucson, AZ 85721. See Goodman et al. 1984.

38. Lynn Rhodes and Nancy Shanklin have a districtwide inservice project focusing on integrating reading and writing in the Denver Public Schools. Like the Albuquerque Project, the Denver Project involves a contract — buying some of the time of each of these university faculty members. While Rhodes and Shanklin work with 125 teachers in this project, they concentrate their daily efforts in twelve classrooms which have been selected as demonstration centers for other teachers in the project and district. During the summer of 1985 they concentrated their inservice effort on kindergarten and first-grade teachers. Several compilations of instructional strategies which teachers might use in their classrooms are available. Contact Nancy Shanklin or Lynn Rhodes, Reading Education, University of Colorado at Denver, Denver, CO 80202. See Rhodes 1981, Shanklin and Rhodes 1989, Clarke 1987.

39. Katherine Au, as part of Project KEEP, has been working to improve reading comprehension in the Kamehameha School. Initially she compared how Hawaiian teachers as opposed to Anglo teachers interacted with Hawaiian children in reading. She then developed instructional lessons in reading capitalizing on, and building from, the natural interaction patterns of the cultures involved. Children in treatment groups made significant progress in reading. Contact Katherine Au, Kamehameha School, Kamehameha Highway, Honolulu, HI. See Au 1980, Au and Mason 1981, Tharp 1982.

Frances Shimotshu has had an ongoing project focused upon improving the teaching of reading and reading comprehension in Chapter I classrooms.

To date this project has made great strides in the area of teaching reading comprehension in multicultural classrooms, and also in the area of parent involvement. Contact Frances Shimotshu, Windward School District, 45–955 Kamehameha Highway, Kaneohe, HI 96744.

40. P. David Pearson, Robert Tierney, and David Tucker have been working with teachers in the Normal, Illinois, area in updating reading comprehension instruction. Their approach has been to meet with teachers and to talk with them about recent research insights in reading and reading comprehension. Teachers in the project then meet and generate what they believe to be instructional strategies which incorporate and build from those insights — testing them out in their classroom, making revisions, and passing them along to other project teachers. Several reports have been made on the Metcalf Project at professional meetings. In some ways this project is a natural extension of a program of prior research on teaching comprehension conducted by P. David Pearson and several of his graduate students. This study demonstrated rather conclusively the effectiveness of accessing children's background information prior to reading. Contact David Tucker in regard to the Metcalf Project, Illinois State University, DeGarmo Hall, Normal, IL 61761. See Gallagher and Pearson 1983; Hansen 1981; Hansen and Pearson 1983; Tierney et al. 1987.

41. Jean Anne Clyde has been involved in a collaborative curriculum study with preschool teachers in a program designed to find out what might be done to highlight preschool reading and writing activities. To date they have developed a set of instructional strategies which teachers might implement in designing more effective literacy environments at this level. Contact Jean Anne Clyde, School of Education, University of Lexington, Lexington, Kentucky. See Clyde 1986.

Harste and Burke worked with Myriam Revel-Wood (Bloomington, Indiana), Mary Lynn Woods (Zionsville, Indiana), and Susan Robinson (Indianapolis) over a three-year period. The focus of this project was the development of a total comprehension-centered reading and writing curriculum for regular elementary school classrooms. These teachers and their classrooms are featured in a videotape series. Contact Jerome Harste, 211 Education Building, Indiana University, Bloomington, IN 47401. See Harste and Jurewicz 1985; Harste, Mitchell-Pierce, and Cairney 1985; Harste, Short, and Burke 1988.

Tony Kring, an elementary school principal, worked with her staff to develop a reading and writing curriculum that reflected recent insights in literacy and literacy learning. Kring began small, working with a single teacher. Success in this room spread throughout the school. Contact Tony Kring, Principal, Indian Meadow School, 4310 Hemstead Road, Fort Wayne, IN 46804.

Katherine Short collaborated with Gloria Kauffman, a first-grade teacher in Goshen, Indiana, to set up a literature-based, comprehension-centered classroom using literature study groups and other instructional techniques to stimulate critical thinking and extensive reading and writing. Although this was initially a single-classroom, year-long project, it has spread to other rooms in the school. Contact Katherine Short, School of Education, Goshen College, Goshen, IN 46526. See Short 1986.

Diane Stephens and Cynthia Brabson have collaborated on how to more effectively integrate writing in the reading program. This project is focused in a special education classroom and is the subject of a dissertation. Contact Diane Stephens, Center for the Study of Reading, 51 Gerty Drive, Champaign, IL 61820. See Stephens 1986.

42. Heidi Mills worked with the early childhood education staff in the Grand Rapids School District to develop a theoretically based reading and writing program for three-, four-, and five-year-olds in a Title I program. Currently an evaluation device is being developed to chart the progress children made over a three-year period. Contact Heidi Mills, School of Education, University of South Carolina, Columbia, SC 29208. See Mills 1986.

Vera Milz (Bloomfield Hills, Michigan) has applied what she has learned about language and language learning to her work in a combination first- and second-grade classroom. Her classroom has become a demonstration center for the school and the nation. Contact Vera Milz, Way Elementary School, 765 East Long Lake Road, Bloomfield Hills, MI. See Milz 1980, 1984.

Scott Paris has had an extensive program of research designed explicitly to teach several cognitive monitoring activities which researchers have found to be associated with successful reading. His program includes classroom support materials which teachers report to be useful in setting up the program. See Paris 1986; Paris, Cross, and Lipson 1984.

43. Dorothy Watson and Kittye Copeland began by forming a teacher support group because of Copeland's frustration in trying to make changes in a district that seemed unsupportive of her efforts. Over the years more and more teachers have joined their support group, which they call TAWL, Teachers Applying Whole Language. To date they have published two books (one elementary and one secondary level) containing strategy lessons which they found successful in moving toward implementing a comprehension-centered reading and writing program. Because of the success of this group, TAWL groups have sprung up all over the country. Currently, national TAWL meetings are held in conjunction with the annual meetings of NCTE and the International Reading Association. Contact Dorothy Watson, 209 Education Building, University of Missouri, Columbia, MO 65211. See Bixby et al. 1984, Huelett 1982.

44. Jane Hansen and Donald Graves currently have a project in which they are working with teachers to implement a process approach to both reading and writing in classrooms. They report significant gains in reading as a function of writing. Contact Jane Hansen or Donald Graves, Morrill Hall, University of New Hampshire, Durham, NH 03824. See Hansen 1987.

45. Bess Altwerger, Virginia Resta, Bonnie Iverson, Mary Ellen Gallegos, and others have been working with Chapter I reading teachers in the Albuquerque Public Schools in setting up a comprehension-centered reading and writing program. Currently Albuquerque Public Schools has contracted with the University of New Mexico to buy one-third of Altwerger's time for her to work with Resta in classrooms and to conduct inservice sessions for Chapter I teachers. As part of this effort, an instructional strategy guide for Chapter I reading teachers has been developed. Contact Virginia Resta, Albuquerque Public Schools, North Area Office, 120 Woodland Northwest, Albuquerque, NM 87107. See Resta 1984.

46. Lucy McCormick Calkins is currently working with teachers in the New York School District to implement a process approach to the teaching of writing. To date, Calkins has made great strides in a district riddled with problems. Contact Lucy McCormick Calkins, Teachers College, Columbia University, New York. See Calkins 1984.

M. Trika Smith-Burke has had an ongoing project to improve the teaching of reading comprehension in the New York Public Schools. This project is one of the first and oldest reading-comprehension-focused inservice efforts in the country. Other projects have grown from the errors as well as the achievements of this project. A series of television programs on reading comprehension was shown to teachers in the New York area in conjunction with this project as part of the series "Sunrise Semester." Contact M. Trika Smith-Burke, Department of Educational Psychology, 933 Shimkin Hall, New York City, NY 10003.

47. Vito Perrone and members of the Center for Teaching and Learning at the University of North Dakota in Grand Forks are the base of the North Dakota Study Group. This group has a long-time interest in the improvement of education as well as teacher education. Lifetime members such as Ruth Gallant and Clara Peterson have worked closely with teachers in North Dakota and other states to those ends. Both the North Dakota Study Group and the Center for Teaching and Learning sponsor a variety of publications of interest to teachers and teacher educators. Their present journal is *Teaching and Learning: The Journal of Naturalistic Inquiry* (Editor, Elizabeth Franklin, Center for Teaching and Learning, University of North Dakota, Grand Forks, ND 58202). See Carini 1979.

48. Charlotte Huck, Gay Su Pinnell, and Diane DeFord have received funding from the state of Ohio to implement Marie Clay's early-intervention reading program in selected first-grade classrooms in the Columbus, Ohio, area. During the first year of this project Marie Clay was brought over from New Zealand to work with project staff in setting up and implementing the project. There are plans to revise as well as extend the project. Contact Gay Su Pinnell, Ohio State University, 219 Arps Hall, 1945 North High Street, Columbus, OH 43210. See Pinnell 1988.

Richard Vacca has been working with teachers in the Cleveland Public Schools to develop an integrated reading and writing program at the elementary and secondary school levels. One component of this project has been to identify effective strategies for teacher change. Contact Richard Vacca, Kent State University, Reading Department, Kent, Ohio. See Vacca 1984.

49. Virginia Pierce has been working with two first-grade teachers in Sherman, Texas, implementing what they call a natural language-learning model of reading and writing in these classrooms. Children in the classrooms made almost two years' gain as compared to children in other first-grade classrooms in the same school. Contact Virginia Pierce, Department of Elementary Education, Austin College, Sherman, TX 75090. See Pierce 1984.

50. Margaret Stevenson, supervisor of language arts for the Edmonton Public Schools, has had an ongoing project to infuse writing in the reading program using the ideas of James Britton and others. She and her staff have made great progress in changing the curriculum of a large school district. Contact Margaret Stevenson, Supervisor, Language Arts, Edmonton Public Schools, 10010-107A Avenue, Edmonton, Alberta T5H OZB.

51. Judith Newman, Olga Scibior, Alan Neilsen, and Andy Manning have been working with teachers in the Halifax area on improving reading and writing instruction in schools. For this purpose they have formed ongoing study groups taking up different topics each year. Teachers in the project have compiled an instructional strategy handbook for elementary teachers. They also have ongoing projects in their classrooms. To date they have worked on areas such as beginning reading and writing, using computers in the language arts classroom, and improving secondary reading instruction. Contact Judith Newman, Olga Scibior, Alan Neilsen, or Andy Manning at Mount Saint Vincent University, Education Department, 166 Bedford Highway, Halifax, Nova Scotia B3M 2J6. See Newman 1982, 1983, 1985.

52. Ethel Buchanan and Orin Cochrane began by providing inservice programs for teachers on how to improve the teaching of reading incorporating recent insights into the process. As they went around the district, they invited teachers to join them in this effort. Once they had a group of committed teachers, they went to the Winnipeg school board and asked to be transferred to an inner-city school with a history of low achievement. Over seven years they transformed this school into a demonstration center for the district. They have begun to sponsor and publish a newsletter entitled *Connections.* Contact Orin Cochrane, Principal, David Livingstone School, 170 Flora Avenue, Winnipeg, Manitoba R2W 2P9. See Buchanan 1980, Cochrane 1985.

53. This analogy was initially made by Kenneth S. Goodman in an address at the 1978 NCTE Language Arts Conference. The text of this address appeared as "The President's Education Program: A Response" in the *SLATE Newsletter* 3 (1978), no. 2: 1–3. For a free copy, send a self-addressed stamped envelope to: SLATE 1978, Membership Service Representative, NCTE, 1111 Kenyon Road, Urbana, IL 61801.

54. Donald Graves initially made this statement in regard to how we teach writing in the United States during a keynote address at the Fall 1979 Language Arts Conference of the National Council of Teachers of English in Hartford, Connecticut. Given the issues and the tendency to seek "quick-fix" solutions, I use the quote here to remind everyone that literacy and critical thinking go hand-in-hand. This holds for children, but also for teachers, researchers, curriculum developers, parents, administrators, and school board members as they go about developing educational policies which see literacy as a potential rather than as a problem.

Bibliography

Adams, M. J., and A. Collins. 1978. A schema-theoretic view of reading. In R. J. Spiro, B. C. Bruce, and W. F. Brewer, eds., *Theoretical issues in reading comprehension.* Hillsdale, N.J.: Erlbaum.

Allington, R. 1984. Content coverage and contextual reading in reading groups. *Journal of Reading Behavior* 16, no. 1: 85–96.

Altwerger, B., and V. Resta. 1985. The Albuquerque Project. Speech given at the Annual Meeting of the International Reading Association, New Orleans.

Anderson, R. C., E. H. Hiebert, J. A. Scott, and I. A. G. Wilkinson. 1985. *Becoming a nation of readers.* Washington, D.C.: U.S. Department of Education.

Anderson, R. C., R. E. Reynolds, D. L. Schallert, and E. T. Goetz. 1977. Framework for comprehending discourse. *American Educational Research Journal* 14, no. 1: 367–81.

Anderson, R. C., R. J. Spiro, and W. E. Montague. 1977. *Schooling and the acquisition of knowledge.* Hillsdale, N.J.: Erlbaum.

Au, K. H. 1980. *A test of the social organizational hypothesis relationship between participation structures and learning to read.* Unpublished doctoral dissertation, University of Illinois at Urbana-Champaign.

Au, K. H., and J. M. Mason. 1981. Social organizational factors in learning to read: The balance of rights hypothesis. *Reading Research Quarterly* 17: 356–97.

Baghban, M. 1984. *Our daughter learns to read and write: A case study from birth to three.* Newark, Del.: International Reading Association.

Barr, B. 1974–75. The effect of instruction on pupil reading strategies. *Reading Research Quarterly* 10, no. 1: 555–82.

Beaugrande, R. de. 1980. *Text, discourse, and process.* Norwood, N.J.: Ablex.

Beaugrande, R. de. 1981. Design criteria for process models of reading. *Reading Research Quarterly* 16, no. 1: 261–315.

Beaugrande, R. de. 1985. *The semiotics of text.* Seminar given at the International Summer Institute of Semiotic and Structural Studies, Indiana University, Bloomington.

Beaugrande, R. de, and W. Dressler. 1981. *Introduction to text linguistics.* New York: Longman.

Bissex, G. 1980. *Gnys at wrk: A child learns to write and read.* Cambridge, Mass.: Harvard University Press.

Bissex, G. 1985. Supporting the writing process. Presentation given at the Annual Meeting of Child-centered Experience-based Learning (CEL), Winnipeg.

67

Bixby, M., S. Crenshaw, P. Crowley, C. Gilles, M. Henricks, D. Pyle, and F. Waters. 1984. *Strategies that make sense: Invitations to literacy for secondary students.* Columbia, Mo.: Teachers Applying Whole Language (1900 Lovejoy Lane, Columbia, MO 65201).

Board, P. 1981. *Valuing the learner in the classroom: Things are not what they seem to be* (Occasional Paper). Tucson, Ariz.: University of Arizona, Program for Language and Literacy.

Boyer, E. L. 1984. *High school: A report on secondary education in America.* New York: Harper.

Brandt, D. 1985. Writer, context, and text. Paper presented as Promising Young Researcher recipient at Annual Meeting of the National Council of Teachers of English, Detroit.

Brown, A. L. 1977. *Knowing when, where, and how to remember: A problem of metacognition* (Technical Report No. 47). Champaign, Ill.: University of Illinois, Center for the Study of Reading.

Brown, A. L. 1981. Metacognitive development and reading. In R. J. Spiro, B. C. Bruce, and W. F. Brewer, eds., *Theoretical issues in reading comprehension.* Hillsdale, N.J.: Erlbaum.

Brown, A. L. 1982. Learning how to learn from reading. In J. Langer and M. Smith-Burke, eds., *Reader meets author: Bridging the gap: A psycholinguistic and sociolinguistic perspective.* Newark, Del.: International Reading Association.

Brown, A. L., and S. S. Smiley. 1977. Rating the importance of structural units of prose passage: A problem of metacognitive development. *Child Development* 48, no. 1: 1–8.

Bruce, B. 1979. *A social interaction model of reading* (BBN Report No. 4238). Champaign, Ill.: University of Illinois, Center for the Study of Reading.

Buchanan, E., ed. 1980. *For the love of reading.* Winnipeg: Whole Language Consultants, Ltd.

Burke, C. L. 1980. A comprehension-centered reading curriculum (videotape). In D. J. Strickler, producer and developer, *Reading comprehension* (videotape series). Portsmouth, N.H.: Heinemann.

Busch, K. M. 1985. A cognitive approach to reading. In A. Crismore, ed., *Landscapes: A state-of-the-art assessment of reading comprehension research, 1974–1984* (Final Report USDE-C-300-83-0130, Volume I). Bloomington, Ind.: Indiana University, Language Education Department.

Bussie, A. M. 1982. "Burn it at the casket": Research, reading instruction, and children's learning of the first R. *Phi Delta Kappan* 60, no. 1: 237–41.

Calkins, L. 1984. *Lessons from a child.* Portsmouth, N.H.: Heinemann.

Carey, R. F. 1980. Empirical vs. naturalistic research? *Reading Research Quarterly* 5: 412–15.

Carey, R. F., ed. In process. *A miscue up-date.* Bloomington, Ind.: ERIC Clearinghouse on Reading and Communication Skills.

Carey, R. F., J. C. Harste, and S. L. Smith. 1981. Contextual constraints and discourse processes: A replication study. *Reading Research Quarterly* 6, no. 1: 201–12.

Carini, P. F. 1979. *The school lives of seven children: A five year study.* Grand Forks, N.D.: North Dakota Study Group.

Cash, J., host. 1984. *Can't read, can't write* (videotape). New York: CBS Broadcasting.

Chall, J. S. 1983. Literacy: Trends and explanations. *Educational Researcher* 12: 3–8.

Christie, F. 1980. *The language development project* (Occasional Papers 1, 2, and 3). Canberra: Curriculum Development Centre.

Clarke, M. 1987. Don't blame the system: Constraints on "Whole Language" reform. *Language Arts* 64: 384–96.

Clyde, J. A. 1986. *A collaborative venture: Exploring the socio-psycholinguistic nature of literacy.* Unpublished doctoral dissertation, Indiana University, Bloomington.

Cochrane, O., D. Cochrane, S. Scalena, and E. Buchanan. 1984. *Reading, writing, and caring.* New York: Richard C. Owens.

Cousin, P. T. 1985. Meeting at the crossroads: Measurement in reading comprehension and in classrooms. In A. Crismore, ed., *Landscapes: A state-of-the-art assessment of reading comprehension, 1974–1984* (Final Report USDE-C-300-83-0130, Volume I). Bloomington, Ind.: Indiana University, Language Education Department.

Crismore, A., ed. 1985. *Landscapes: A state-of-knowledge assessment of reading comprehension instructional research, 1974–1984* (Final Report USDE-C-300-83-0130, Volume I). Bloomington, Ind.: Indiana University, Language Education Department.

Dahl, K. 1984. *Reading and writing as a transactional process.* Unpublished doctoral dissertation, Indiana University, Bloomington.

Dahl, K., and B. Roberts. 1985. Exemplary studies for teachers to use. In A. Crismore, ed., *Landscapes: A state-of-the-art assessment of reading comprehension research, 1974–1984* (Final Report USDE-C-300-83-0130, Volume I). Bloomington, Ind.: Indiana University, Language Education Department.

DeFord, D. 1981. Literacy: Reading, writing and other essentials. *Language Arts* 58: 652–58.

DeLawter, J. 1970. *Oral reading errors of second grade children exposed to two different reading approaches.* Unpublished doctoral dissertation, Teachers College, Columbia University.

Dijk, T. van. 1976. *Pragmatics of language and literature.* Amsterdam: North Holland Publishing.

Dijk, T. van. 1977. Semantic macro-structures and knowledge frames in discourse comprehension. In M. A. Just and P. A. Carpenter, eds., *Cognitive processes in comprehension.* Hillsdale, N.J.: Erlbaum.

Dijk, T. van. 1979. *Macro-structures.* Hillsdale, N.J.: Erlbaum.

Dillon, G. L. 1978. *Language processing and the reading of literature: Toward a model of comprehension.* Bloomington, Ind.: Indiana University Press.

Downing, J. 1970. Children's concepts of language in learning to read. *Educational Researcher* 12, no. 1: 106–12.

Downing, J. 1979. Cognitive clarity and linguistic awareness. Paper presented at the International Seminar on Linguistic Awareness and Learning to Read, University of Victoria, Canada.

Durkin, D. 1978–79. What classroom observations reveal about reading comprehension instruction. *Reading Research Quarterly* 14, no. 1: 481–533.

Dyson, A. H. 1984. Learning to write/learning to do school: Emergent writers' interpretations of school literacy tasks. *Research in the Teaching of English* 10: 233–64.

Eckland, B. K. 1982. College entrance examination trends. In G. R. Austin and H. Garber, eds., *The rise and fall of national test scores,* 9–34. New York: Academic Press.

Edelsky, C., et al. 1984. *A language deficit theory for the 80's: CALP, BICS, and Semilingualism* (mimeographed). Tempe, Ariz.: Arizona State University, Elementary Education.

Eisner, E. W. 1985. *The art of educational evaluation: A personal view.* London: Falmer Press.

Erickson, F. 1984. School literacy, reasoning, and civility: An anthropologist's perspective. *Review of Educational Research* 54, no. 4: 525–46.

Erickson, F. 1985. Qualitative research on teaching. In M. C. Wittrock, ed., *Handbook of research in teaching* (3rd Edition). New York: Macmillan.

Farr, R., and R. Carey. 1986. *Reading: What can be measured?* (2nd Edition). Newark, Del.: International Reading Association.

Farr, R., and L. Fay. 1982. Reading trend data in the United States: A mandate for caveats and caution. In G. R. Austin and H. Garber, eds., *The rise and fall of national test scores.* New York: Academic Press.

Farr, R., L. Fay, and H. H. Negley. 1978. *Reading achievement in Indiana (1944–45 and 1976): Then and now.* Bloomington, Ind.: Indiana University, Language Education.

Ferreiro, E., and A. Teberosky. 1982. *Literacy before schooling* (Trans. by K. Goodman Castros). Portsmouth, N.H.: Heinemann.

Flores, B., E. Garcia, S. Gonzales, G. Hidalgo, K. Kaczmarck, and T. Romero. 1985. *Bilingual instructional strategies.* Tempe, Ariz.: Arizona State University, Bilingual Research Center.

Franklin, B. 1984. *A naturalistic study of literacy in bilingual classrooms.* Unpublished doctoral dissertation, Indiana University, Bloomington.

Gallagher, M. C., and P. D. Pearson. 1983. Fourth grade students' acquisition of new information from text. Paper presented at the National Reading Conference, Austin.

Gambrell, L. B. 1984. How much time do children spend reading during teacher-directed reading instruction? In J. A. Niles and L. A. Harris, eds., *Changing perspectives on research in reading/language processing and instruction* (34th Yearbook of NRC). Rochester, N.Y.: National Reading Conference.

Gollasch, F. V., ed. 1982a. *Language and literacy: The selected writings of Kenneth S. Goodman* (Volume 1: Process, Theory, Research). London: Routledge & Kegan Paul.

Gollasch, F. V., ed. 1982b. *Language and literacy: The selected writings of Kenneth S. Goodman* (Volume 2: Reading, Language, and the Classroom Teacher). London: Routledge & Kegan Paul.

Goodlad, J. L. 1984. *A place called school: Prospect for the future.* Boston, Mass.: McGraw-Hill.

Goodman, K. S. 1965. A linguistic study of cues and miscues in reading. *Elementary English* 42: 639–43.

Goodman, K. S. 1969. Analysis of oral reading miscues: Applied psycholinguistics. *Reading Research Quarterly* 4, no. 1: 9–30.

Goodman, K. S. 1979. Bridging the gaps in reading: Respect and communication. In J. C. Harste and R. F. Carey, eds., *New perspectives on comprehension* (Monographs in Language and Reading Studies). Bloomington, Ind.: Indiana University, School of Education Publications.

Goodman, K. S. 1983. The solution is the risk: A reply to the report of the National Commission on Excellence in Education. *SLATE Newsletter* 9, no. 1: 1–4.

Goodman, K. S. 1984a. Tests as discriminatory devices. Presentation given during the Proffit Lecture Series on Education, Indiana University, Bloomington.

Goodman, K. S. 1984b. Unity in reading. In A. C. Purves and O. Niles, eds., *Becoming readers in a complex society* (Part 1: 83rd Yearbook of the National Society for the Study of Education). Chicago: University of Chicago Press.

Goodman, K. S., and Y. M. Goodman. 1979. Learning to read is natural. In L. B. Resnick and P. A. Weaver, eds., *Theory and practice of early reading* (Volume 2). Hillsdale, N.J.: Erlbaum.

Goodman, Y. M., and C. L. Burke. 1980. *Reading strategies: Focus on comprehension.* New York: Holt, Rinehart & Winston.

Goodman, Y. M., D. Watson, and C. Burke. 1986. *Reading miscue inventory* (2nd Edition). New York: Richard C. Owens.

Goodman, Y. M., S. Wilde, L. Bird, S. Vaughan, W. Kasten, and D. Weatherill. 1984. *A two-year case study observing the development of third and fourth grade native American children's writing processes* (Final Report NIE-G-81-0127). Tucson, Ariz.: University of Arizona, Program in Language and Literacy, Arizona Center for Research and Development.

Green, J., and D. Bloome. 1983. Ethnography and reading: Issues, approaches, criteria, and findings. In J. Niles and L. Harris, eds., *New inquiries in reading research and reading instruction* (32nd Yearbook of NRC). Rochester, N.H.: National Reading Conference.

Guba, E., and Y. S. Lincoln. 1985a. *The countenances of fourth generation evaluation: Description, judgment, and negotiation* (mimeographed). Bloomington, Ind.: Indiana University, School of Education, Inquiry Program Area.

Guba, E., and Y. S. Lincoln. 1985b. *Do inquiry paradigms imply inquiry methodologies?* (mimeographed). Bloomington, Ind.: Indiana University, School of Education, Inquiry Program Area.

Halliday, M. A. K. 1973a. *Explorations in the functions of language.* London: Edward Arnold.

Halliday, M. A. K. 1973b. Foreword. In P. Mackey and P. Schaub, eds., *Breakthrough to literacy.* Glendale, Calif.: Bowmar.

Halliday, M. A. K. 1974. *Language and social man.* London: Longman.

Halliday, M. A. K. 1978. *Language as social semiotic.* London: Edward Arnold.

Hansen, J. 1981. The effects of inference training and practice on young children's reading comprehension. *Reading Research Quarterly* 16, no. 1: 391–417.

Hansen, J. 1987. Organizing student learning: Teachers teach what and how. In J. Squire, ed., *The dynamics of language learning.* Urbana, Ill.: National Conference on Research in English and the ERIC Clearinghouse on Reading and Communication Skills.

Hansen, J., and D. Graves. 1984. Implementing a process approach to reading and writing in classrooms. Speech given at the Annual Meeting of the American Educational Research Association, New Orleans.

Hansen, J., and P. D. Pearson. 1983. An instructional study: Improving the inferential comprehension of good and poor fourth grade readers. *Journal of Educational Psychology* 75: 821–29.

Harnischfeger, A., and D. E. Wiley. 1975. *Achievement test score decline: Do we need to worry?* Chicago: Central Midwest Regional Laboratory (CEM-REL).

Harste, J. C. 1980. Reading and writing: The instructional connection (videotape). In D. J. Strickler, director and producer, *Reading comprehension* (videotape series). Portsmouth, N.H.: Heinemann.

Harste, J. C. 1985a. Becoming a nation of language learners: Beyond risk. In J. C. Harste and D. Stephens, eds., *Toward practical theory: A state of practice assessment of reading comprehension instruction* (Final Report, USDE-C-300-83-0130, Volume II). Bloomington, Ind.: Indiana University, Language Education Department.

Harste, J. C. 1985b. Portrait of a new paradigm: Reading comprehension research. In A. Crismore, ed., *Landscapes: A state-of-the-art assessment of reading comprehension research, 1974–1984* (Final Report USDE-C-300-83-0130, Volume I). Bloomington, Ind.: Indiana University, Language Education Department.

Harste, J. C. 1988. What it means to be strategic: Good readers as informants. *Reading Canada* 6, no. 1: 28–36.

Harste, J. C., and C. L. Burke. 1977. A new hypothesis for reading teacher education research: Both the teaching and learning of reading are theoretically based. In P. D. Pearson, ed., *Reading: Research, theory and practice* (26th Yearbook of NRC). Rochester, N.Y.: National Reading Conference.

Harste, J. C., C. L. Burke, and V. A. Woodward. 1981. *Children, their language and world: Initial encounters with print* (Final Report NIE-G-79-0132). Bloomington, Ind.: Indiana University, Language Education Department.

Harste, J. C., and R. F. Carey. 1979. Comprehension as setting. In J. C. Harste and R. F. Carey, eds., *New perspectives in comprehension* (Monographs in Language and Reading Studies). Bloomington, Ind.: Indiana University, School of Education Publications.

Harste, J. C., and R. F. Carey. 1985. Classrooms, constraints, and the language process. In J. Flood, ed., *Promoting reading comprehension.* Newark, Del.: International Reading Association.

Harste, J. C. (developer and host), and E. Jurewicz (producer and director). 1985. *The authoring cycle: Read better, write better, reason better* (videotape series). Portsmouth, N.H.: Heinemann.

Harste, J. C., and L. J. Mikulecky. 1984. The context of literacy in our society. In A. C. Purves and O. Niles, eds., *Becoming readers in a complex society* (Part 1: 83rd Yearbook of the National Society for the Study of Education). Chicago: University of Chicago Press.

Harste, J. C., K. Mitchell-Pierce, and T. Cairney. 1985. *The authoring cycle: A viewing guide.* Portsmouth, N.H.: Heinemann.

Harste, J. C., K. G. Short, and C. L. Burke. 1988. *Creating classrooms for authors: The reading-writing connection.* Portsmouth, N.H.: Heinemann.

Harste, J. C., and D. Stephens, eds. 1985. Toward practical theory: A state-of-practice assessment of reading comprehension instruction (Final Report USDE-C-300-83-0130, Volume II). Bloomington, Ind.: Indiana University, Language Education Department.

Harste, J. C., and D. Stephens, eds. In process. *Teaching reading comprehension as inquiry.* Portsmouth, N.H.: Heinemann.

Harste, J. C., V. A. Woodward, and C. L. Burke. 1984. *Language stories and literacy lessons.* Portsmouth, N.H.: Heinemann.

Heath, S. B. 1983. *Ways with words.* Cambridge, England: Cambridge University Press.

Heath, S. B. In press. Critical thinking: An anthropological view. In P. D. Pearson and M. Kamil, eds. *Handbook of Reading Research.* White Plains, N.Y.: Longman.

Heine, D. 1985. Using background knowledge. In A. Crismore, ed., *Landscapes: A state-of-the-art assessment of reading comprehension research, 1974–1984* (Final Report USDE-C-300-83-0130, Volume I). Bloomington, Ind.: Indiana University, Language Education Department.

Herzfeld, M. 1983. Signs in the field. *Semiotica* 4, no. 1: 91–106.

Hill, M. 1980. *Parenting and language education: A theoretical view of parental role in children learning to read and write.* Unpublished doctoral dissertation, Indiana University, Bloomington.

Holdaway, D. 1979. *The foundations of literacy.* Portsmouth, N.H.: Heinemann.

Huelett, J., ed. 1982. *Whole language activities for a comprehension centered language program.* Columbia, Mo.: Teachers Applying Whole Language (1900 Lovejoy Lane, Columbia, MO 65201).

Irwin, J. W., and C. Davis. 1980. Assessing readability: The checklist approach. *Journal of Reading* 24, no. 1: 124–30.

Iser, W. 1978. *The act of reading: A theory of aesthetic response.* Baltimore, Md.: Johns Hopkins Press.

Jaggar, A., and M. T. Smith-Burke. 1985. *Observing the language learner.* Newark, Del.: International Reading Association.

Jenkins, P. W. 1980. *The language learning of a language delayed child: A phenomenological study.* Unpublished dissertation, University of Missouri, Columbia.

Jensen, J. M., ed. 1984. *Composing and comprehending.* Urbana, Ill.: National Conference on Research in English and the ERIC Clearinghouse on Reading and Communication Skills.

Johnston, P. H. 1983. *Reading comprehension assessment: Cognitive basis.* Newark, Del.: International Reading Association.

Johnston, P. H. 1987. Assessing the process, and the process of assessment, in language arts. In J. Squire, ed., *The dynamics of language learning.* Urbana, Ill.: National Conference on Research in English and the ERIC Clearinghouse on Reading and Communication Skills.

King, M. 1985. The natural curriculum (videotape). In E. Jurewicz (producer and director) and J. Harste (developer and host), *The authoring cycle: Read better, write better, reason better.* Portsmouth, N.H.: Heinemann.

Kintsch, W. 1977. On comprehending stories. In M. A. Just and P. A. Carpenter, eds., *Cognitive processes in comprehension.* Hillsdale, N.J.: Erlbaum.

Kintsch, W., and T. van Dijk. 1978. Toward a model of text comprehension and production. *Psychological Review* 85, no. 1: 363–94.

Kirsch, I., and J. T. Guthrie. 1985. Adult reading practices for work and leisure. Paper presented at the Annual Meeting of the National Reading Conference, St. Petersburg.

Kozol, J. 1985. *Illiterate America.* New York: Anchor Press/Doubleday.

Kucer, S. 1983. *A message based model of discourse production.* Unpublished doctoral dissertation, Indiana University, Bloomington.

Langer, J. A. 1985. The construction of meaning and the assessment of comprehension: An analysis of reader performance on standardized test items. In R. Freedle, ed., *Cognitive and linguistic analyses of standardized test items.* Norwood, N.J.: Ablex.

Langer, J. A., and G. M. Pradl. 1984. Standardized testing: A call for action (Position Paper prepared for the Commission on Reading of the National Council of Teachers of English). *Language Arts* 61: 764–67.

Lindfors, J. W. 1980. *Children's language and learning.* Englewood Cliffs, N.J.: Prentice Hall.

Magoon, A. J. 1977. Constructivist approach to educational research. *Review of Educational Research* 47: 657–93.

Martin, B., and P. Brogan. 1971. *Teacher's guide to instant readers.* New York: Holt.

Mattingly, I. G. 1972. Reading, the linguistic process, and linguistic awareness. In J. F. Kavanagh and I. G. Mattingly, eds., *Language by ear and by eye: The relationship between speech and reading.* Cambridge, Mass.: MIT Press.

Mattingly, I. G. 1979. Reading, linguistic awareness, and language acquisition. Paper presented at the International Seminar on Linguistic Awareness and Learning to Read, University of Victoria, Canada.

McCracken, R., and M. McCracken. 1979. *Reading, writing, and language.* Winnipeg: Pegius Publishers, Ltd.

Meek, M. 1982. *Learning to read.* London: Bodley Head.

Mikulecky, L. J. 1981. *Job literacy: The relationship between school preparation and workplace ability* (Final Report NIE-G-79-0168). Bloomington, Ind.: Indiana University, Language Education Department.

Mills, H. 1986. *Writing evaluation: A transactional process.* Unpublished dissertational research, Indiana University, Bloomington.

Milz, V. 1980. The comprehension-centered classroom: Setting it up and making it work. In D. J. Strickler and B. P. Farr, eds., *Reading comprehension: Resource guide.* Portsmouth, N.H.: Heinemann.

Milz, V. 1984. *A psycholinguistic description of the development of writing in selected first grade students.* Unpublished doctoral dissertation, University of Arizona.

Mischler, E. G. 1979. Meaning in context: Is there any other kind? *Harvard Educational Review* 49: 1–19.

Murray, J. 1984. *Dialogue as semiosis: Paulo Freire's Adult Literacy Program* (mimeographed). A paper given at the Annual Meeting of the Semiotic Society of America, Bloomington, Ind.

National Assessment of Educational Progress. 1985. *The reading report card: Progress toward excellence in our schools: Trends in reading over four national assessments, 1971–1984.* Princeton, N.J.: Educational Testing Service.

National Commission on Excellence in Education. 1983. *A nation at risk: The imperative for educational reform.* Washington, D.C.: U.S. Department of Education.

Neilsen, A. R., B. J. Rennie, and A. M. Connell. 1982. Allocation of instructional time to reading comprehension and study skills in intermediate grade social studies classrooms. In J. A. Niles and L. A. Harris, eds., *New inquiries in reading research and instruction* (32nd Yearbook of NRC). Rochester, N.Y.: National Reading Conference.

Newman, J. M. 1983. *Whole language: Translating theory into practice* (Monographs on Learning and Teaching). Halifax: 15 Braeside Lane, Halifax, NS B3M 3J6.

Newman, J. M. 1985. *Whole language: Theory in use.* Portsmouth, N.H.: Heinemann.

Newman, J. M., ed. 1982. *Whole language activities.* Halifax: 15 Braeside Lane, Halifax, NS B3M 3J6.

Northcutt, N. 1975. *Adult Functional Competency: A Summary* (mimeo). Austin, Tex.: University of Texas.

Nueraka, E. 1982. *SAT scores and reading performance.* Unpublished doctoral dissertation, Wayne State University.

Odell, L. 1980. Business writing: Observations and implications for teaching composition. *Theory into Practice* 19: 225–32.

Paris, S. G. 1986. Teaching children to guide their reading and learning. In T. E. Raphael, ed., *Contexts of school-based literacy.* New York: Longman.

Paris, S. G., D. R. Cross, and M. Y. Lipson. 1984. Informed strategies for learning: A program to improve children's reading awareness and comprehension. *Journal of Educational Psychology* 76: 1239–52.

Pearson, P. D., ed. 1984. *Handbook of reading research.* New York: Longman.

Pearson, P. D., and R. J. Tierney. 1984. Reading like a writer. In A. C. Purves and O. Niles, eds., *Becoming readers in a complex society* (Part 1: 83rd Yearbook of the National Society for the Study of Education). Chicago: University of Chicago Press.

Pierce, V. L. 1984. *Bridging the gap between language research/theory and practice: A case study.* Unpublished doctoral dissertation, Texas Woman's University.

Pinnell, G. S. 1985. The Ohio Early Literacy Project. Presentation given at the Annual Meeting of the International Reading Association, New Orleans.

Pinnell, G. S. 1988. Holistic ways to help children at risk of failure. *Teachers Networking* 9, no. 1: 1, 10–13.

Psacharopoulos, G. 1981. Return to education: An updated international comparison. *Comparative Education* 17, no. 1: 321–41.

Ravitch, D. 1985. *The schools we deserve: Reflections on the educational crises of our time.* New York: Basic Books.

Research Department, International Reading Association. 1984. *Responding to "A nation at risk": Appraisal and policy guidelines.* Newark, Del.: International Reading Association.

Resta, V., ed. 1984. *Chapter I reading instructional strategies guide for North Area elementary Chapter I reading teachers.* Albuquerque, N.M.: Albuquerque Public Schools North Area Office (120 Woodland N. W., Albuquerque, NM 87107).

Rhodes, L. K. 1978. *The interaction of beginning readers' strategies and tests reflecting alternate models of predictability.* Unpublished doctoral dissertation, Indiana University, Bloomington.

Rhodes, L. K. 1979. Comprehension and predictability: An analysis of beginning reading materials. In J. C. Harste and R. F. Carey, eds., *New perspectives in comprehension* (Monographs in Language and Reading Studies). Bloomington, Ind.: School of Education Publications.

Rhodes, L. K. 1981. I can read! Predictable books as resources for reading and writing instruction. *Reading Teacher* 34, no. 1: 511–29.

Rhodes, L. K., ed. 1981. *Children's literature: Activities and ideas* (Volume 1). Denver, Colo.: University of Colorado, Reading Education.

Rosen, H. 1985. *Stories and their meaning.* London: National Association for the Teaching of English.

Rosenblatt, L. 1969. Toward a transactional theory of reading. *Journal of Reading Behavior* 10, no. 1: 31–43.

Rosenblatt, L. 1978. *The reader, the text, the poem.* Carbondale, Ill.: Southern Illinois University Press.

Rowe, D. W. 1985a. The big picture: A quantitative meta-analysis of reading comprehension research. In A. Crismore, ed., *Landscapes: A state-of-the-art assessment of reading comprehension research, 1974–1984* (Final Report

USDE-C-300-0130, Volume I). Bloomington, Ind.: Indiana University, Language Education Department.

Rowe, D. W. 1985b. A guided tour of the landscapes: Research on reading comprehension instruction. In A. Crismore, ed., *Landscapes: A state-of-the-art assessment of reading comprehension research, 1974–1984* (Final Report USDE-C-300-0130, Volume I). Bloomington, Ind.: Indiana University, Language Education Department.

Rowe, D. W., and J. C. Harste. 1985a. Reading and writing in a system of knowing. In M. R. Sampson, ed., *The pursuit of literacy: Early reading and writing.* Dubuque, Iowa: Kendall/Hunt.

Rowe, D. W., and J. C. Harste. 1985b. Surveying the landscapes: Plans and procedures for the research. In A. Crismore, ed., *Landscapes: A state-of-the-art assessment of reading comprehension research, 1974–1984* (Final Report USDE-C-300-83-0130, Volume I). Bloomington, Ind.: Indiana University, Language Education Department.

Rumelhart, D. E. 1977. Toward an interactive model of reading. In S. Dornie, ed., *Attention and performance* (Volume VI). Hillsdale, N.J.: Erlbaum.

Rumelhart, D. E., and A. Ortony. 1977. The representation of knowledge in memory. In R. C. Anderson, R. J. Spiro, and W. E. Montague, eds., *Schooling and the acquisition of knowledge.* Hillsdale, N.J.: Erlbaum.

Scibior, O. 1987. *Reconsidering spelling development: A socio-psycholinguistic perspective.* Unpublished doctoral dissertation, Indiana University, Bloomington.

Seminoff, N., K. K. Wixson, and C. W. Peters. 1984. Reading redefined: A Michigan Reading Association position paper. *Michigan Reading Journal* 17, no. 1: 4–7.

Shanklin, N. 1981. *Relating reading and writing: Development of a transactional theory of the writing process* (Monographs in Language and Reading Studies). Bloomington, Ind.: Indiana University, School of Education Publications.

Shanklin, N., and L. Rhodes. 1985. The Denver Project. Speech given at the Center for the Expansion of Language and Thinking (CELT) Rejuvenation Conference, Bloomington, Ind.

Shanklin, N., and L. Rhodes. 1979. Transforming literacy instruction: A university–public school collaboration. *Educational Leadership* 46 (March): 58–61.

Shanklin, N., and R. Vacca. 1985. *Shifts in teacher beliefs about writing and writing instruction.* Speech given at the Annual Meeting of the National Reading Conference, St. Petersburg.

Sherman, B. 1979. Reading for meaning. *Learning* 60, no. 1: 41–44.

Short, K. G. 1985. A new lens for reading comprehension: Comprehension processes as critical thinking. In A. Crismore, ed., *Landscapes: A state-of-the-art assessment of reading comprehension instruction* (Final Report USDE-C-300-83-0130, Volume I). Bloomington, Ind.: Language Education Department.

Short, K. G. 1986. *Literacy as a collaborative experience.* Unpublished doctoral dissertation, Indiana University, Bloomington.

Shuy, R. W. 1979. On the relevance of recent developments in sociolinguistics to the study of language, learning, and early education. In O. Garcia and M. King, eds., *Language, children, and society.* Oxford: Pergamon Press.

Siegel, M. 1983. *Reading as signification.* Unpublished doctoral dissertation, Indiana University, Bloomington.

Smith, D. M. 1984. Premises underlying a new methodology for educational research. Paper presented at the Annual Meeting of LARS, New York University, New York.

Smith, F. 1971. *Understanding reading* (1st Edition). New York: Holt.

Smith, F. 1978. *Understanding reading* (2nd Edition). New York: Holt.

Smith, F. 1982. *Writing and the writer.* New York: Holt.

Smith, F. 1984. *Essays in literacy.* Portsmouth, N.H.: Heinemann. (See particularly "The language arts and the learner's mind" and "Demonstrations, engagement, and sensitivity.")

Smith, F. R., and K. M. Feathers. 1983. Teacher and student perceptions of content area reading. *Journal of Reading* 26, no. 1: 348–54.

Smith, K., C. Edelsky, B. Flores, and R. Peterson. 1985. The Arizona Project. Presentation given at the Annual Meeting of the International Reading Association, New Orleans.

Smith, S. L. 1980. Retelling as measures of comprehension: A perspective. In J. C. Harste and R. F. Carey, eds., *New perspectives in comprehension* (Monographs in Language and Reading Studies). Bloomington, Ind.: Indiana University, School of Education Publications.

Smith, S. L. 1982. Learning strategies of mature college learners. *Journal of Reading* 26, no. 1: 5–12.

Smith-Burke, M. T. The STAR Project (Personal communication).

Snyder, S. 1985a. Legitimizing teachers' insights. In J. Harste and D. Stephens, eds., *Toward practical theory: A state-of-practice assessment of reading comprehension instruction* (Final Report USDE-C-300-0130, Volume II). Bloomington, Ind.: Indiana University, Language Education Department.

Snyder, S. 1985b. Teachers as explorers: Teacher-researchers and present research needs. In A. Crismore, ed., *Landscapes: A state-of-the-art assessment of reading comprehension research, 1974–1984* (Final Report USDE-C-300-83-0130). Bloomington, Ind.: Indiana University, Language Education Department.

Spiro, R. J. 1977. Remembering information from text: The state of schema approach. In R. C. Anderson, R. J. Spiro, and W. E. Montague, eds., *Schooling and the acquisition of knowledge.* Hillsdale, N.J.: Erlbaum.

Spiro, R. J., B. C. Bruce, and W. F. Brewer, eds. 1980. *Theoretical issues in reading comprehension.* Hillsdale, N.J.: Erlbaum.

Steffel, N. 1985. *Nurturing literacy: A curriculum for parents of newborn to three-year-old children.* Unpublished doctoral dissertation, Indiana University, Bloomington.

Stephens, D. 1985a. Toward a reconception of educational inquiry. *Forum* 2: 1–11.

Stephens, D. 1985b. Uncharted land: Reading instruction with the special education student. In A. Crismore, ed., *Landscapes: A state-of-the-art assessment of reading comprehension, 1974–1984* (Final Report USDE-C-300-83-0130, Volume I). Bloomington, Ind.: Indiana University, Language Education Department.

Stephens, D. 1986. *The integration of reading and writing: A collaborative study of change in a special education classroom.* Unpublished doctoral dissertation, Indiana University, Bloomington.

Stephens, D., and J. C. Harste. 1986. Accessing the potential of the learner: Toward an understanding of the complexity of context. *Journal of Special Education* 20, no. 1: 67–72.

Sternglass, M., and S. L. Smith. 1984. *Retrospective accounts of language and learning processes* (Grant-in-aid Final Report). Bloomington, Ind.: Indiana University, Research and Graduate Development.

Stevenson, H. W. 1984. *Making the grade: School achievement in Japan, Taiwan, and the United States* (Annual Report). Stanford, Calif.: Center for Advanced Study in the Behavioral Sciences.

Stitch, T. 1983. Literacy in non-school settings. Symposium presentation at the Annual Meeting of the National Reading Conference, Austin.

Stitch, T. 1985. Avoid "quick-fix" solutions to illiteracy. *The Wall Street Journal,* August 31, Education Supplement, p. 2.

Suhor, C. 1984. Towards a semiotics-based curriculum. *Journal of Curriculum Studies* 16, no. 3: 247–57.

Taylor, D. 1983. *Family literacy: Young children learning to read and write.* Portsmouth, N.H.: Heinemann.

Teale, W. H. 1978. What studies of early readers tell us. *Language Arts* 55: 922–32.

Teale, W. H. 1982. Toward a theory of how children learn to read and write naturally. *Language Arts* 59: 555–70.

Tharp, R. G. 1982. The effective instruction of comprehension: Results and descriptions of the Kamehameha Early Education Program. *Reading Research Quarterly* 17: 503–37.

Thorndike, R. L. 1973. *Reading comprehension education in fifteen countries: An empirical study.* New York: Wiley.

Tierney, R. J., and J. LaZansky. 1981. The rights and responsibilities of readers and writers: A contractual agreement. *Language Arts* 16: 252–67.

Tierney, R. J., P. D. Pearson, and D. Tucker. 1984. The Metcalf Project. Presentation given at the Annual Meeting of the Conference on Reading Research, Anaheim.

Tierney, R. J., D. L. Tucker, M. Gallagher, P. D. Pearson, and A. Crismore. 1987. The Metcalf Project: A teacher-researcher collaboration in developing reading and writing instructional problem-solving. In J. Samuels and P. D. Pearson, eds., *Changing school reading programs: Principles and case studies.* Newark, Del.: International Reading Association.

Vacca, R. T. 1984. Elementary teachers' level of use and adaptation of writing process strategies. Paper given at the Annual Meeting of the National Reading Conference.

Vygotsky, L. S. 1978. *Mind in society: The development of higher psychological processes.* Cambridge, Mass.: Harvard University Press.

Wells, G. 1981. *Learning through interaction: The study of language development* (Volume 1: Language at Home and at School). Cambridge, England: Cambridge University Press.

Wells, G. 1985. *Storying across the curriculum.* Presentation given at the Annual Conference of Child-centered Experience-based Learning (CEL), Winnipeg.

Wells, G., S. Barnes, and J. Wells. 1984. *Linguistic influences on educational attainment* (Final Report). Toronto: Ontario Institute for Studies in Education.

Wertsch, J. 1979. From social interaction to higher psychological processes. *Human Development* 22, no. 1: 1–22.

Winograd, P. N. 1983. *Strategic difficulties in summarizing texts* (Technical Report No. 153). Champaign, Ill.: University of Illinois, Center for the Study of Reading.

Winograd, P. N., V. C. Hare, R. Garner, P. A. Alexander, and J. Haynes. 1984. *When lookbacks fail.* Paper presented at the Annual Meeting of the American Educational Research Association, New Orleans.

Winograd, P. N., and P. Johnston. 1982. Comprehension monitoring and the error detection paradigm. *Journal of Reading Behavior* 14, no. 1: 61–76.

Yaden, D., and S. Templeton, eds. 1985. *Metalinguistic awareness and beginning literacy.* Portsmouth, N.H.: Heinemann.

Author

Jerome C. Harste, professor of language education at Indiana University, has been an elementary school teacher, a Peace Corps volunteer, and chair of the NCTE Commission on Reading. His volume *Language Stories and Literacy Lessons*, with Drs. Carolyn Burke and Virginia Woodward, won the 1988 David H. Russell Research Award for distinguished contributions to the teaching of English. Dr. Harste is currently a member of the NCTE Commission on Curriculum and the editorial boards of the *Reading Research Quarterly* and *Research in the Teaching of English.* He is past president of the National Reading Conference, a member of the board of directors of the International Reading Association, and president-elect of the National Conference on Research in English.